DATE DUE

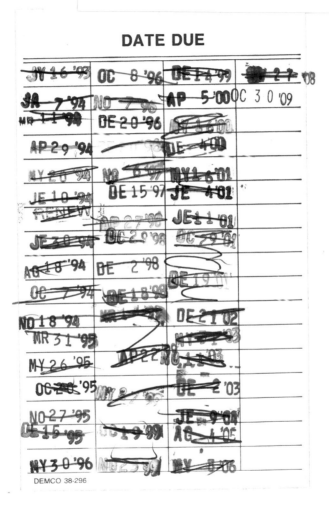

JY 16 '93	OC 8 '96	DE 14 99	MY 27 '08
JA 7 '94	NO 7 '96	AP 5 '00	OC 30 '09
MR 11 '94	DE 20 '96	MY 16 '00	
AP 29 '94		DE 4 '00	
MY 20 '94	NO 6 '97	MY 16 '01	
JE 10 '94	DE 15 '97	JE 4 '01	
RENEW	DE 27 '98	JE 11 '01	
JE 20 '94	OC 29 '98	OC 29 '01	
AG 18 '94	DE 2 '98		
OC 7 '94	DE 18 '98	DE 19 '01	
NO 18 '94	MR 11 '99	DE 21 '02	
MR 31 '95		MY 9 '03	
MY 26 '95	AP 22 '99	NO 11 '03	
OC 20 '95	MY 27 '99	DE 2 '03	
NO 27 '95		JE 9 '04	
DE 15 '95	OC 19 '99	AG 4 '05	
MY 30 '96	NO 23 '99	MY 8 '06	

DEMCO 38-296

STEP FORWARD

STEP FORWARD

Sexual Harassment in the Workplace

What You Need to Know!

S U S A N   L .   W E B B

M A S T E R M E D I A

MASTERMEDIA and colophon are registered trademarks
of MasterMedia Limited

Library of Congress Cataloging-in-Publication Data
Webb, Susan L.
    Step forward : sexual harassment in the workplace : what you need
to know / Susan L. Webb.
        p.   cm.
    ISBN 0-942381-51-2
    1. Sexual harassment of women.   2. Sexual harassment.   I. Title.
HD6060.3.W43   1992
331.4'133—dc20   92-2715
                                                             CIP

Production services by Martin Cook Associates, Ltd.
Manufactured in the United States of America

10 9 8 7 6 5 4 3

To Glenn,
my husband, best friend, and business partner,
who makes my life complete

Contents

Acknowledgments

I would like to thank the people who contributed to this book, all in their own unique way: Leise Robbins, who gave me my first chance to work in the training business and encouraged me all the way; Virginia Sweet Lincoln, who sat with me one day eleven years ago at the House of Pancakes and told me how to get started; Pat Watkins, whose kind and supportive words about my work were some of the first positive comments I heard and came at a much-needed time; Don Bennett, who so thoughtfully lets me know now and then that I'm on the right track; Howard Shenson, the marketing genius, who's always willing to share his expertise and insight; Dorothy C. Bullitt, who gave me those little pushes along the way and helped me go in the right direction; and Kathleen Andersen, who helped me just keep going period, when the road got blackest.

And thanks to those clients and friends who make my work so enjoyable and rewarding: Joyce Cameron of Burger King Corporation; Rich Williamson of the U.S. Forest Service; Chief Donald Manning of the Los Angeles Fire Department; Jim Baxter of Alcoa Aluminum; Dave Andrews of Perkins, Coie; Emily Jarosz of East Bay Municipal Utility District; Bev King of the Los Angeles Department of Water and Power; and my two special friends TJ and CM.

To my brother, Mark, for standing with me always; my parents, Bob and Kathryn Webb, for giving me all they had to give—my father, who taught me so much so early, and my mother, who helped me keep learning by sending me to college; my grandfather, Raymond Hansford, the gentlest man I've ever known, and my grandmother, Myrtle Hansford, always whistling the "Missouri Waltz," who gave me the sweetest times and the sweetest memories of my life.

To those involved in my day-to-day work in the area of sexual harassment: Melinda Affronte, who was there at the beginning, willing to help in any way; Barrie Russell, printer extraordinaire, who provides high-quality work without losing patience; Christine Yateman, our office manager, without whom we simply could not function at all; and, most of all, Glenn Shoate, business manager/visionary/adviser, who took us these last few steps over the last three years to make this book possible.

To Susan Stautberg for literally making this book happen with her persistence, enthusiasm, and, as said by many others before me, her vision.

And finally, thanks to Professor Anita Hill and all the other women and men who have the courage to stand up for themselves and for us all, in the face of anger, disbelief, ignorance, and prejudice.

Preface by Eleanor Raynolds, CBE

Thanks to Clarence Thomas and Anita Hill, the entire subject of sexual harassment has been brought to everyone's attention. Women are remembering questionable incidents (even blatant ones), while men are wondering, what is sexual harassment? In fact, some men feel that women ask for privileged behavior. Women, on the other hand, want to be treated as business colleagues, just as men are treated by one another. Women wish to be known for their accomplishments, not for their dress, hairdo, or shapely figure. It is difficult enough for women in business; now they are thinking about how they can perform better to avoid harassment altogether.

Harassment is more likely to occur in jobs that are at the lower staff levels. Secretaries, waitresses, and assistants all have to deal with different types of harassment daily, and tend to take no notice of it at all. However, we are beginning to see changes. Recently three executives at Hal Riney & Partners were accused of sexual harassment. Two of these people were men, one a woman. The complaint further accuses the head of the agency of "creating a hostile work environment which condones and fosters sexual harassment," according to *Adweek* magazine. Will this be the beginning of many lawsuits?

Clearly, sexual harassment has been a taboo subject. The

Thomas–Hill hearing has enabled people to discuss openly situations that they personally encountered even ten to fifteen years ago. It is therefore understood by many why Anita Hill kept silent for many years. There are women from a variety of career backgrounds who have kept embarrassing situations to themselves. Wanting to move ahead, not wanting to cause problems or scenes, women have been quiet. Perhaps this terrible incident, which has had an effect on both men and women, will be positive in the long run.

As women learn to treat each other better, men will treat women as business colleagues, not as their mothers, wives, girlfriends, etc. Women must begin to listen to the opinions of other women, value their work, hold them in high regard. Women should mentor, educate not only their own daughters but their co-workers as to the value of a woman's work, her opinions, her integrity. Women must lose the fear of associating with other women—standing firm together even though their male colleagues have radically different ideas. Yes, as women treat other women with dignity, I can assure you, men will do the same.

Every company in the United States needs to understand what harassment really is. Both men and women in the workplace want to know what is right and what is wrong. This book will be a "must" on every human resources professional's desk and, in fact, should be given to every single senior officer with P & L responsibility. It is key for all of us to know how to create the best possible environment for our people. We are all part of the solution; we can make the difference, and Susan Webb's book will help.

Eleanor Raynolds is a partner at Ward Howell International and coauthor of Beyond Success.

Introduction

There are approximately 100 million grown women in the United States, and I thought I heard them all growling today . . . these days women take it very seriously when they're not taken seriously.

—JOHN CHANCELLOR, *NBC Nightly News* commentary

During the Thomas–Hill sexual harassment controversy, women were indeed growling, very loudly, and wanting themselves and this issue to be taken seriously. But men were growling too, and for the same reasons. The refrain that "men just don't get it" simply isn't true. *Some* men don't get it, but many men do. And those who get it are the men who growled and complained right along with the women.

The sooner we all realize that this is an issue that affects both men and women, wives and husbands, sons and daughters, mothers and fathers, the better off we'll be. Someone jokingly said the other day, using an opening line from the old *Adventures of Superman* television series, that resolving sexual harassment issues fairly is about "truth, justice, and the American way." I agree. Now if we could just figure out what that way is. Sometimes the way is hard to find.

The sooner we realize the magnitude of the sexual harassment problem, the better off we'll be, too. When my office first began publishing a newsletter on sexual harassment, *The Webb Report,* in January of 1985, one concern was whether we could find enough information to fill a newsletter that was published every other month. That concern quickly vanished as we were flooded with clippings, articles, and phone calls from across the country, and we moved to publishing on a monthly basis.

Before long we were hearing from people around the world—Japan, Sweden, Australia, England, Canada, the Dominican Republic—and our problem in publishing *The Webb Report* became one of choosing what to put in and what had to be left out of each newsletter. And now, with the allegations raised by Anita Hill, our office is swamped with calls, requests, and an influx of information about complaints, incidents, and stories of sexual harassment.

The latest studies and surveys show essentially the same results they've shown for the last fifteen years—that 40 to 50 percent of working women, and up to 15 percent of working men, experience sexual harassment. In October 1991 the National Association for Female Executives polled its 1,300 members and found that 53 percent said they were sexually harassed by people who had power over their jobs or careers. Fully 64 percent didn't report the harassment, and more than half of those who did report it said that the problem wasn't resolved to their satisfaction.

Also in October 1991, Professor James Gruber of the University of Michigan–Dearborn released findings of his three-year study of 650 women in Estonia, Finland, Sweden, the Soviet Union, and Michigan. The study showed that nearly 50 percent of all working women experience sexual harassment, with its most common form being repeated requests for dates and sexually suggestive remarks. A poll conducted by the *New York Times* during the Thomas hearing showed similar results—that approximately 40 percent of working women say they have been sexually harassed.

Those of us working in the area of harassment knew the problem was there all along, and we knew how big the problem was. Now it's just getting the national and international attention it deserves.

From Canada

In September 1991, Member of Parliament William Kempling from Burlington, Ontario, offered an apology to Liberal deputy leader Sheila Copps for having called her a "slut" during a Commons debate: "I lost my temper and said something I should not have said." But Kempling didn't explain why he originally had insisted that he had said "what a pain in the butt." He said, "What is most important is that my choice of words has offended the honorable member and also has offended the temper of the House."

Copps accepted the apology, but, according to some, the issue is a symbol of what's wrong between male and female parliament members in the House of Commons. Liberal leader Jean Chretien said, "We are disturbed by the number of incidents of this nature that are occurring all the time."

Halifax MP Mary Clancy, who speaks for the Liberals on women's issues, said that the time has come for men to truly examine the kind of invective that is hurled at women MPs. "The words are probably unimportant, but the emotion that they're expressing is an emotion of hatred, an emotion of exclusion, an emotion that women are not supposed to be here."

From Europe

Suzanne Moore, writer for London's *The Independent,* opened her column titled "That Male Urge to Tell Women What to Think" with more stinging words: "So, in the end, Clarence Thomas was given what the pundits have called the 'benefit of the doubt.' In other words, he benefited and Professor Hill was doubted." She said that "the Republicans have got their way, the Supreme Court has got a black judge, CNN has got another feather in its cap. But what have women got from this affair?" Her answer: "not a lot."

However, some action against harassment is being taken in both Britain and Brussels. Guidelines have been introduced by Britain's Trades Union Congress that state that "sexual harassment can include leering, ridicule and embarrassing remarks" and that it can also involve "compromising invitations, demands for sexual favors, sexual assault, remarks about dress or appearance, abuse, offensive use of pin-ups, pornographic pictures, or repeated physical contact."

Two reporters, Terry Pattinson and Rory Watson, wrote in *The European* that thanks to legislation and the work of the Equal Opportunities Commission, the British Trades Union Congress, and the National Council for Civil Liberties, "men now realise that their behavior can lead to disciplinary charges and even dismissal." They say that the days when victims had to put up with the harassment or quit their jobs are gone forever.

In Brussels, Vasso Papandreou, the Greek Social Affairs Commissioner and only woman among seventeen commissioners, has taken the lead in establishing Europewide rules to eliminate sexual harassment in the workplace. The commission states that "sexual attention becomes sexual harassment if it is persisted in once it has been made clear that it is regarded by the recipient as offensive, although one incident of harassment may constitute sexual harassment if sufficiently serious."

From Japan

In response to questions at a news conference prompted by the Thomas hearing, Japan's top government spokesman said that Japan isn't prepared to ban sexual harassment. The chief cabinet secretary, Misoki Sakamoto, said that sexual harassment is not a major problem in Japan, though "all people need to exercise caution."

There was no Japanese term for the problem of harassment until several years ago, when the Japanese borrowed from English and coined the term *seku-hara*. Now, according to a survey released in August 1991 by the Santama Group to Consider Sexual Discrimination at Work, about 70 percent of Japanese women say they have experienced some type of sexual harassment on the job. The most common problem experienced by the 6,500 working women surveyed was a "failure to be recognized as full human beings." They were referring to the almost universal expectation of Japanese businesses that women will serve tea, clean their male colleagues' desks, and perform other menial jobs—regardless of their job description—and tolerate demeaning comments without protest. About 60 percent of the women said they had been fondled or forced to listen to sexual jokes or descriptions of sexual experiences. More than 90 percent said they were sexually harassed while commuting to and from work.

In Washington, D.C., congressional hearings were held in September 1991 to investigate allegations of sexism and racism in Japanese companies doing business in the United States. One American female employee who plans to leave her job with a Japanese-owned and -managed international trading firm said, "Sexual harassment is considered almost something of a joke to the Japanese." She told of pornographic calendars embossed with the corporate seal and of weekly visits to the office by a video porn peddler catering to the Japanese executives.

When Tom Lantos, the subcommittee chairman, asked the company president to explain meetings at which only Japanese employees were allowed, the president explained that the purpose of the meetings was not to talk shop. "We're isolated from Tokyo by seven thousand miles. We talk about chicks and that kind of subject." Talk about somebody who doesn't get it! The list goes on and on.

And at Home

The first sexual harassment workshop I conducted was for thirty men in the Street and Sewer Maintenance Division of a public works department. They called it the "good ol' boy department." It was early 1981, and they were actually interested in hearing about sexual harassment—nobody knew too much about it then.

Five years later I was to conduct a workshop in another company for a similar group. When I went up to the front of the training room, one of the men had taped a tampon, colored with red ink so it looked bloody, to the overhead projector. When I asked him why, he said he'd heard that I was a bitch. That was a bad day. They were not willing to listen to anything that anyone had to say about sexual harassment.

Last week I conducted a training session in which the employees actually applauded when I told them that my book on sexual harassment was being published, and they were fairly receptive to the information about harassment. So I've seen interest in sexual harassment run the gamut, from high interest to outright hostility to support and understanding.

But the problem that bothers me the most is that in all these workshops, whether in 1981 or 1991, the same questions keep coming up over and over. The lack of knowledge and understanding about sexual harassment is appalling and sometimes discouraging to anyone who works in the field. There is so much more work to do even to make a dent in the problem.

So What About Now?

A few years ago, my dad and my brother were in the business of making stairs, doors, and door openers for storm shelters (a fairly lucrative business where they live, in Oklahoma, an area known as "tornado alley"). When business would get slow, my brother would jokingly say to me that what they needed was a real bad tornado—not one that would hurt anybody, just one that would scare people so they'd go out and build more storm shelters.

A few years later, my brother started a different business, manufacturing and selling safes for collectors and people with valuables who want to store them at home. You can probably guess what comes next. When business gets slow, my brother calls me up and laughs and says that what he needs is a real big burglary—not one in which anyone gets hurt, but one that convinces people they need to buy a safe. It has become our standing joke: tornado or burglary, take your pick.

When the Thomas–Hill controversy occurred, my phone rang a lot. One evening it was my brother calling. Knowing what was bound to be happening with my sexual harassment business, he laughed and said, "Well, Sis, I guess you finally got your real bad tornado, huh?"

How true. But the problem with the Thomas–Hill tornado, and with any other sexual harassment storm, is that people always get hurt. She did, he did, their families did; even you and I, as individuals and as a nation, hurt from that storm.

The sooner we realize that it affects us all and that we all must play a part in solving this problem, the sooner we will be rid of it. I hope this book helps us all.

Seattle
November 1991

STEP FORWARD

1

The History of Sexual Harassment: How We Got to This Point

Not long ago I was conducting a sexual harassment workshop and we were waiting for everyone to come in and sit down so we could get started. A man in the front row turned to the woman sitting next to him and said loudly and, I thought at the time, jokingly, "What the hell are we doing here? I don't know what the stink's all about. Ten years ago you never heard anything about sexual harassment. Now there's something in the paper every damn day!"

He got no reaction, so he went on. "I wish I could get someone to sexually harass *me*. I've been trying for years to get someone to sexually harass me, and no one will do it." Then he burst out laughing.

The woman he was talking to looked upset and embarrassed, and apparently she didn't believe, know, or care whether or not he was joking. After his second statement, about wanting someone to harass him, she delivered her comeback, telling him in some detail exactly why she thought no one would ever bother to sexually harass him, emphasizing his lack of appeal and other not-so-endearing characteristics. That was the end of their discussion.

Actually, he was right—in the first part of his comments, at least: for the most part, ten years ago most of us hadn't heard much about sexual harassment, and now there is something in the paper almost every day. The truth is it's just a very, very old problem, getting a lot of new attention.

Many people who are facing the issue of sexual harassment for the first time today have little or no knowledge of how we got to this point. A bit of historical background can go a long way in helping us see the overall picture of sexual harassment and understand the intricacies of this complex and troubling problem.

Court records as far back as American colonial times show examples of what we today call sexual harassment. According to Charles Clark in the August 1991 *CQ Researcher,* it was in 1734 that a group of female servants published a notice in the *New York Weekly Journal* that said, "We think it reasonable we should not be beat by our mistresses' husbands, they being too strong and perhaps may do tender women mischief." Strikingly similar examples were reported in Canadian court records (Toronto, 1915) and in Genesis 39 (in which the harasser was female and the victim of harassment was male).

According to Clark, in the 1960s the basis for today's awareness of sexual harassment fell into place:

- Women began entering (and staying in) the work force in large numbers. In 1959 there were 22 million women in the work force, or approximately 33 percent; by 1991 there were 57 million working women, or 45.5 percent of the American work force.

- The 1964 Civil Rights Bill was passed, which broadened the employment-discrimination section, Title VII, to cover sex discrimination.
- The birth control pill, the women's movement, and the sexual revolution began changing society's views of men, women, work, and family.

THE 1970s

"The 1970s ushered in an era of dramatic efforts to curb workplace discrimination of all forms," says Clark. In 1972 Congress passed the Equal Employment Opportunity Act, giving the federal Equal Employment Opportunity Commission (EEOC) an independent general counsel appointed by the president. This counsel was given the authority to bring cease-and-desist orders and to sue in federal court those employers guilty of workplace discrimination. Also in 1972, Congress passed the Education Act Amendments prohibiting sex discrimination at schools and universities that receive any federal funding.

But it was well into the 1970s, actually ten years after the enactment of the Civil Rights Act, when federal courts heard the first cases in which sexual harassment was the primary complaint. In these cases (*Miller* v. *Bank of America, Corne* v. *Bausch & Lomb, Inc., Barnes* v. *Train*) the courts interpreted sexual harassment based on sex as a "personal matter" between the two individuals, and not as actions directed at or affecting groups of people. Thus, these cases were not successful in establishing sexual harassment as a form of sex discrimination.

In the very first case (*Corne* v. *Bausch & Lomb, Inc.*), two female employees resigned because of repeated verbal and physical advances by their supervisor. The district court refused to hold the company liable because the supervisor's conduct served no employer policy and didn't benefit the employer. The court called the supervisor's conduct "a personal proclivity, peculiarity or mannerism."

But in 1976 a case (*Williams* v. *Saxbe*) finally did establish a cause of action for sexual harassment. The court ruled that the behavior in question had only to create an "artificial barrier to employment that was placed before one gender and not the other, even though both genders were similarly situated." Thus, conditions of employment that were applied differently to men and women, such as sexual harassment, were forbidden under Title VII as sex discrimination. This was a major and landmark decision in beginning to address sexual harassment in the workplace.

These early sexual harassment cases involved claims that the plaintiffs had been deprived of tangible job benefits for their failure to succumb to sexual advances (*Tomkins* v. *Public Service Gas & Electric*). The women had to show that there was a clear relationship between the objectionable conduct (the harassment) and the negative employment consequences (being fired or demoted, given distasteful job assignments or poor performance reviews). If they could not show these tangible, negative consequences, then the harassing behavior was seen as isolated sexual misconduct, not a Title VII violation (*Hill* v. *BASF Wyandotte Corp.*, *Neely* v. *American Fidelity Assurance Co.*, *Davis* v. *Bristol Laboratories*).

In 1977 the first charge of sexual harassment of students was brought under Title IX of the 1972 Education Act Amendments. A female undergraduate at Yale University said that her professor offered her an A in his course if she would accept his sexual proposition and that when she refused she got a C. In her suit (*Alexander* v. *Yale University*) she demanded that the lower grade be removed from her record; she was joined in this demand by four other students and a faculty member.

The district court maintained that sexual harassment may constitute sex discrimination under Title IX, stating, "It is perfectly reasonable to maintain that academic advancement conditioned upon submission to sexual demands constitutes sex discrimination in education, just as questions of job retention or promotion tied to sexual demands from supervisors have become increasingly recognized as potential violations of Title VII's ban against sex discrimination in employment."

Her suit was dismissed in 1980 because she had graduated from Yale and in the meantime the university had established a sexual harassment grievance procedure for dealing with complaints. However, the importance of this case is that it served to define sexual harassment in the educational system and bring attention to teacher-student types of harassment.

In addition to the rush of legal activity taking place in the seventies, a number of major studies and surveys were published. Lin Farley's book, *Sexual Shakedown: The Sexual Harassment of Women on the Job* (1978), defined the problem and told story after story of women who experienced harassment at work. Catharine A. MacKinnon wrote *Sexual Harassment of Working Women: A Case of Sex Discrimination* (1979) and argued the legal remedies. Even anthropologist Margaret Mead contributed, with an article, titled "A Proposal: We Need Taboos on Sex at Work," that is still quoted today.

THE 1980s

What seemed to be a quiet start for the 1980s was truly a noisy beginning. In November 1980, during the final days of the Carter Administration, EEOC's Guidelines on Discrimination Because of Sex were formalized by chairman Eleanor Holmes Norton. The Guidelines had been published earlier in the spring of that year and subject to public discussion and debate. In the fall they became official.

It was in the early eighties that the first district court decision allowed for a suit over an "atmosphere of discrimination" (*Brown* v. *City of Guthrie*). While the woman could not show loss of tangible job benefits, she did establish that the harassment created a hostile, offensive, and unbearable work environment. The *Brown* court was the first to cite the EEOC Guidelines on Discrimination Because of Sex, quoting Section A, that sexual harassment is a violation of Title VII when "such conduct has the purpose or effect of substantially interfering with an individual's work performance or creating an intimidating, hostile, or offensive work environment."

Shortly after *Brown,* in *Bundy* v. *Jackson* (1981), the circuit court ruled on the basis of the atmosphere of discrimination, and cited the Guidelines to support its opinion. The court interpreted "terms and conditions of employment" protected by Title VII to mean more than tangible compensation and benefits.

Other courts, however, did not follow the pattern of *Brown* and *Bundy.* In *Hill,* the district court had held that no action under Title VII for sexual harassment was available where the plaintiff did not show that her success and advancement depended on her agreeing to her supervisor's demands. The court observed that Title VII should not be interpreted as reaching into sexual relationships that arise during the course of employment but do not have a "substantial effect" on that employment.

Then, in 1982 and 1983, two federal circuit courts of appeal adopted their own classification scheme for sexual harassment cases, identifying two basic varieties of sexual harassment: (1) "Harassment in which a supervisor demands sexual consideration in exchange for job benefits ('quid pro quo')" and (2) "harassment that creates an offensive environment ('condition of work' or 'hostile environment' harassment)" (*Henson* v. *City of Dundee* and *Katz* v. *Dole*).

Quid pro quo ("this for that") harassment, as defined by the courts, encompasses all situations in which submission to sexually harassing conduct is made a term or condition of employment or in which submission to or rejection of sexually harassing conduct is used as the basis for employment decisions affecting the individual who is the target of such conduct.

In the typical quid pro quo harassment case, an employee (or prospective employee) is approached by an individual with the power to affect the employee's employment future and asked for sexual consideration in return for a job benefit or in order to avoid losing a job benefit.

The *Henson* court stated four elements that a plaintiff must prove to establish a case of quid pro quo sexual harassment:

- He or she belongs to a protected group, i.e., is a male or female.
- He or she was subjected to unwelcome sexual harassment.
- The harassment complained of was based on sex.
- The employee's reaction to harassment complained of affected tangible aspects of the employee's compensation, terms, conditions, or privileges of employment.

Condition of work or *hostile environment* sexual harassment, as defined by the courts, is roughly equivalent to the third category of sexual harassment listed in the EEOC Guidelines: unwelcome and demeaning sexually related behavior that creates an intimidating, hostile, and offensive work environment. In the *Henson* case, the circuit court reversed the lower court's holding that the plaintiff must show some tangible job detriment in addition to the hostile work environment created by sexual harassment. The court said that although not every instance or condition of work environment harassment gives rise to a Title VII claim, a plaintiff who can prove a number of elements can establish a claim. These elements are similar to those for quid pro quo harassment also outlined by *Henson*:

- The employee belongs to a protected group under Title VII, i.e., is a man or a woman.
- The employee was subjected to unwelcome sexual harassment.
- The harassment complained of was based on sex.
- The harassment complained of affected a term, condition, or privilege of employment.
- The employer knew or should have known of the harassment in question and failed to take prompt remedial action.

The U.S. Supreme Court Decision on Sexual Harassment

On June 19, 1986, the U.S. Supreme Court ruled that sexual harassment on the job is illegal discrimination even if the victim suffers no economic loss. The Court held that "the language of Title VII is not limited to 'economic' or 'tangible' discrimination" and the law's phrase "terms, conditions or privileges" of employment indicates congressional intent to "strike at the entire spectrum of disparate treatment of men and women," including harassment that creates a hostile work environment.

The Court quoted the *Henson* court, saying, "Sexual harassment which creates a hostile or offensive environment for members of one sex is every bit the arbitrary barrier to sexual equality at the workplace that racial harassment is to racial equality. Surely, a requirement that a man or woman run a gauntlet of sexual abuse in return for the privilege of being allowed to work and make a living can be as demeaning and disconcerting as the harshest of racial epithets."

The Court reiterated that not all workplace behavior that may be defined as harassment can be said to affect terms or conditions of employment. For sexual harassment to be actionable it must be sufficiently severe or pervasive to "alter the conditions of the victim's employment and create an abusive working environment."

The Court's key holdings were:

- Sexual harassment is a form of sex discrimination illegal under Title VII of the 1964 Civil Rights Act.
- Sexual harassment is illegal even if the victim suffered only a hostile work environment and not the loss of economic or tangible job benefits.
- Employers are not automatically liable for sexual harassment by their supervisors.
- Lack of knowledge of the harassment does not automatically relieve the employer of liability for supervisors' harassment.
- The complainant's consent to the behavior does not relieve the employer of liability. The question is not the "voluntariness" of the complainant's participation, but whether her conduct indicated that the behavior was unwelcome.
- The complainant's behavior, such as provocative speech and dress, may be considered in determining whether the complainant found particular sexual advances unwelcome.

Since then, other courts have continued to define and refine the definition of what constitutes sexual harassment. The courts' answers to this question have, for the most part, become somewhat predictable and followed a pattern parallel to that of racial harassment.

While some people believed (or hoped) that the courts would narrow the scope of what they consider discriminatory sexual harassment, this has not been the case. Actually, the opposite has occurred: initial rulings limited the scope of what was defined as harassment, and subsequent rulings broadened the definition.

THE 1990s

In the 1990s the problem of sexual harassment has continued to get widespread attention. On March 19, 1990, the EEOC issued updated Guidelines on sexual harassment, reflecting decisions made by the agency itself as well as by various courts since the first Guidelines were issued in 1980.

A number of studies and surveys have also been conducted and their results published. In September 1990, the Pentagon released the largest military survey ever on sexual harassment, showing that of 20,000 military respondents worldwide, 64 percent of the women and 17 percent of the men said that they had been sexually harassed. In a separate study (1991), the Navy revealed that of the 6,700 they surveyed, 75 percent of the women and 50 percent of the men responding said that sexual harassment occurs within their commands.

In the business world, estimates continue to run from 15 to 40 percent of women and 14 to 15 percent of men who experience sexual harassment. On campuses, the estimates range from 40 to 70 percent of female students experiencing harassment, with most harassment coming from other students.

The number of complaints filed with the EEOC has shown a general upward trend over the years (1981, 3,456; 1982, 4,233; 1983, 4,385; 1984, 4,380; 1985, 4,953; 1986, 4,431; 1987, 5,336; 1988, 5,215; 1989, 5,204; 1990, 5,557). However, these numbers don't reveal much about the problem, because many harassment victims sue privately and don't go through the EEOC at all.

Pinups and Sexual Harassment:
Robinson *v.* Jacksonville Shipyards

Already in the nineties, two landmark court decisions have been delivered. In the first (*Robinson* v. *Jacksonville Shipyards*, January 1991), the Sixth U.S. Circuit Court of Appeals in Florida ruled that nude pinups in the workplace can constitute sexual harassment. In this case, a female shipyard welder accused her employer of sexual harassment and won, with the court ruling that posting pictures of nude and partly nude women is a form of sexual harassment.

In other cases, courts have found that pornographic pictures may contribute to an atmosphere of sexual harassment. But *Robinson* is thought to be the first finding that such pictures are sexual harassment in and of themselves.

The federal district court judge in Jacksonville, Florida, Howell Melton, said that the employer, Jacksonville Shipyards, Inc., and two of its employees were directly liable for the harassment, and rejected what he called their "ostrich defense." The company claimed that it had been unaware of many of the woman's complaints.

The judge said that the shipyard maintained a boys' club atmosphere with a constant "visual assault on the sensibilities of female workers." The pictures included pinup calendars and close-ups of female genitals posted on the walls. The judge went on to say that the sexualized atmosphere of the workplace had the effect of keeping women out of the shipyard.

The opinion also said, "A pre-existing atmosphere that deters women from entering or continuing in a profession or job is no less destructive to and offensive to workplace equality than a sign declaring 'men only.' " Judge Melton ordered the shipyard to institute a sexual harassment policy written by the National Organization for Women's Legal Defense and Education Fund. NOW, the New York–based women's advocacy group, had brought the case to trial.

The decision found both verbal and visual sexual harassment, and described thirty pornographic pictures displayed at the shipyard. One was of a woman's pubic area with a spatula pressed against it. Some of the pictures came from calendars provided by tool companies and included one of a nude woman bending over with her buttocks and genitals exposed. Another showed a frontal view of a female torso with the words "U.S.D.A. Choice" written on it. The verbal harassment included explicit sexual remarks.

The decision said that when the woman told her co-workers that their behavior was sexual harassment, they took that as a new subject of ridicule and denied that they were harassing her. Two other female employees testified that they were also subjected to sexual harassment, in the form of remarks, pinches, and sexual teasing.

According to the testimony, the female welder complained repeatedly to her supervisors about the pictures. At one meeting when she complained, a supervisor told her that the company had no policy against the pictures and that the men had "constitutional rights" to post them, so he would not order them removed. According to the ruling, the shipyard had no system for recording sexual harassment complaints and supervisors had no instructions to document such complaints.

The judge ordered the shipyard to pay her legal fees but did not order it to pay back pay for time lost from work. The woman said that she had missed workdays because of the strain of the harassment, but the judge said that her estimates of missed days were too vague. Under Title VII, no other damages are available.

In this case, expert-witness testimony about sexual stereotyping was used. Based on the testimony, the judge said that the women were subject to "sex role spillover," whereby women are evaluated by co-workers and supervisors based on the women's sexuality and sexual worth rather than their value as workers.

Alison Wetherfield of the NOW Legal Defense and Education Fund said, "Judge Melton understands how damaging and illegal it is for women workers to be given the message that they are welcome at work only so long as they accept the stereotypical role of sex object. . . . The decision recognizes the impossible position many harassed women are in, in a very sensitive and unusual way."

According to the decision, women are still rare in this shipyard's skilled jobs, with only 6 women among 846 men employed as skilled craft workers in 1986. The company has never employed a woman in a supervisory position such as foreman, leadman, or quarterman.

A year after the suit was filed the company had instituted a sexual harassment policy forbidding employees to make any kind of sexual conduct a condition of employment or to create an intimidating, hostile, or offensive work environment (as per the EEOC Guidelines). The policy was posted on bulletin boards, but the employees received no training in connection with them. The court ruled that the policy had little or no effect on what it said was a sexually hostile work environment and that the company did not adequately communicate the new policy to employees.

The latest policy, ordered by the court, called for the offensive pictures to be removed and for workers to be educated about sexual harassment. It provided for penalties, including warnings, suspensions, and firings, for those who violate the policy.

The Reasonable-Woman Decision: Ellison v. Brady

Then, on January 23, 1991, a second and more even important landmark ruling was made by the Ninth U.S. Circuit Court of Appeals in San Francisco. This case, *Ellison* v. *Brady*, has serious implications with regard to investigating and resolving complaints. In its ruling, the court established a new legal standard, called the "reasonable woman" standard. This case is especially important to employers, not only because of the expanded definition of sexual harassment, but also because the court indicated that it expects swift and decisive actions in response to harassment in the workplace.

In *Ellison*, the employer's response to the harassment was to repeatedly counsel the harasser, instructing him to leave the woman alone, and to transfer him to a different facility for four months—a response that many employers would characterize as appropriate. In fact, before *Ellison* went to the federal court, the EEOC had held that the employer, the Internal Revenue Service, was not liable because it had taken sufficient steps to remedy the situation.

Nevertheless, the court disagreed. It found fault with the employer's not consulting the victim about the harasser's return to the office, for not reprimanding the man with probation, suspension, or some other type of discipline, and finally for transferring the woman to avoid further conflict, even though she had requested the transfer.

The court also said that in some cases the mere presence of an employee who has harassed a co-worker may create a hostile work environment, so that the only reasonable recourse is to discharge the harasser. The *Ellison* decision suggests that managers take preventive steps to protect themselves, their organizations, and their employees:

- Develop a clear sexual harassment policy statement and grievance procedures, spelling this out in the employee manual.
- Tell employees that harassment is taken from the victim's perspective, so employees should be sensitive to the feelings and viewpoints of their co-workers.
- Treat sexual harassment as a serious employee infraction,

taking prompt and remedial action to correct the situation. If harassment continues, the harasser should be disciplined by suspension, demotion, or some other form of concrete punishment.

- Include the victim in determining the appropriate action, at least when consideration is being given to allowing the harasser to work alongside the victim.
- Do not alter the terms or conditions of the victim's employment when responding to the incidents of harassment.
- Consider whether the harasser must be terminated because his or her mere presence creates a hostile work environment for the victim.
- Show that the severity of conduct varies inversely with the frequency of the conduct.

The court also said:

- An understanding of the victim's perspective requires an analysis of the different perspectives of men and women.
- A female employee may state a *prima facie* case of hostile environment sexual harassment by alleging conduct that a reasonable woman would considered sufficiently severe; however, the employer does not have to accommodate the idiosyncrasies of the rare hypersensitive employee.
- The reasonable-woman standard is not static but will change over time as the views of reasonable women change.
- There can be unlawful sexual harassment even when harassers do not realize that their conduct creates a hostile working environment.

In this case, Kerry Ellison, the plaintiff, was an agent for the IRS office in San Mateo, California. Sterling Gray, who worked about twenty feet from her, asked her out for lunch one day in

June 1986, and they went out to eat. A few months later Gray asked her out again, for drinks and lunch, and Ellison refused and made it clear that she was not interested. Gray then started to write her love letters.

In an October 1986 note scribbled on a message pad, he wrote, "I cried over you last night and I'm totally drained today." She continued to refuse his advances, which he made in person and in writing, and finally asked a co-worker to tell Gray to leave her alone—all to no avail. A few days later he wrote a three-page, single-spaced letter, saying "I know that you are worth knowing with or without sex. . . ."

Ellison said she was frightened by his attentions and "frantic" about what he might do next. She filed a complaint with her employer, alleging sexual harassment. Gray was counseled, instructed to leave Ellison alone, and eventually transferred to another location. Three months later he was allowed to return to Ellison's office under two conditions: that he complete additional training for a month at another location and that he leave Ellison alone when he returned.

Ellison was not consulted about Gray's transfer or the conditions of his return. When Ellison learned that Gray was returning to her workplace, she requested and received a transfer. Then she filed suit.

The trial court federal judge dismissed the case, applying the "reasonable person" test to the circumstances and ruling that Gray's actions were "isolated and genuinely trivial." The judge ruled that the average adult, regardless of sex, would not have found Ellison's workplace hostile. But the appeals court reversed that decision and threw out the reasonable-person rule. The court ruled that a hostile work environment must be judged from the perspective of the victim—in this case, the "reasonable woman."

This means that the victim's feelings must play a crucial role in identifying a series of actions as sexual harassment and that many employers will have to adopt a broader perspective in addressing sexual harassment complaints. Supervisors, especially male supervisors, may no longer disregard complaints because they do not find the behavior offensive; it is the victim's perception that must be taken into account.

According to attorney Steven Winterbauer, *Ellison* "marks a significant departure from the prevailing standard governing claims of sexual harassment. The Ninth Circuit has joined a growing minority of courts taking an increasingly aggressive stance against workplace harassment. This trend appears to be a good indication of the future development of employment law."

According to Alice Kahn of the *San Francisco Chronicle*, "The case has helped reverse a 154-year-old legal convention of determining sexual harassment based on what is known as the 'reasonable man' (more recently the 'reasonable person') standard. This [the old standard] says that determination of harassment is based on what the court believes a reasonable man would think."

Still, there is much work to be done. Consider these three cases:

- According to 9-to-5, the National Association for Working Women, an Atlanta woman reported on the association's hotline that her harassment case was dismissed after a photo of the defendant's wife was introduced. According to 9-to-5, "The judge ruled the plaintiff was too unappealing to compete with the wife."
- In May 1991, Dr. Frances Conley, one of the country's premier female neurosurgeons, quit her twenty-five-year teaching post at Stanford University, saying that male surgeons caressed her legs under the operating table, called her "honey," and blamed her debating style on premenstrual

syndrome. Dr. Conley said that she had put up with snide comments and unwelcome touching because she feared that speaking up would cost her her job, but when she learned that students were complaining of the same sexual harassment, she could no longer keep quiet.

· In an August 1991 survey by the *Syracuse Herald American*, one company's personnel coordinator wrote, "The reason there has never been a harassment charge filed [at this company] is because this is a male oriented company and it wouldn't be worth the trouble. 'Sexual harassment is usually brought on by cute and/or flirty girls' seems to be the attitude. The harassment you would receive for filing a complaint just wouldn't be worth it."

It's not necessary that you study this chapter in depth, but it is difficult to fully understand and appreciate the gravity of sexual harassment without some awareness of how the issue came to be what it is today. Even though sexual harassment is a very old problem, it continues to be troubling, complex, and extraordinarily damaging.

CHAPTER SUMMARY

Sexual harassment is not a new problem, but one that goes back thousands of years.

The first sexual harassment cases heard by the courts, in the 1970s, involved only those in which the victim had lost tangible job benefits such as pay, promotions, job assignments, or even the job itself, because of the harassment.

In the fall of 1980 the EEOC issued its Guidelines on Discrimination Because of Sex, saying that sexual harassment is a form of sex discrimination and should be treated the same as other forms of illegal discrimination.

In the early 1980s the first court decision was made that allowed for an "atmosphere of discrimination" whereby an employee was subjected to harassment "interfering with an individual's work performance or creating an intimidating, hostile, or offensive work environment."

In 1982 and 1983 two courts made the distinction between quid pro quo (tangible job benefits) harassment and "hostile environment" harassment.

The one Supreme Court case involving sexual harassment was heard in 1986, and validated what other courts had said in previous rulings about sexual harassment.

In the 1990s more attention has been focused on the problem of sexual harassment, by court rulings about pinups at work and the reasonable-woman standard, and by allegations of harassment against public officials.

2

Defining and Understanding Sexual Harassment

A few years ago, a pertinent story appeared in the "Slice of Life" column of my local newspaper. ("Slice of Life" is where amusing, silly, or funny little stories are reported for everyone's daily amusement.) In this story, the woman, who worked for a rapid transit authority as a token clerk, claimed that she was subjected to continuous and repeated sexual comments by the general public because of an advertising poster that was behind her work station.

The poster advertised a health club with the caption "Have we got two great figures for you!" The first great figure was the $19.95 they charged to join the club, and the second was "Miss Pin-Up of 1983," lying on her side in a very small string bikini.

When I read the story, I, like most people, thought it was amusing and a little trivial, and I couldn't help thinking that some people—like this woman—really push the limits, that we were getting to the point where everything in the world is considered sexual harassment.

A few months later I heard another interesting story, this one about a pizza parlor whose employees had to wear animal costumes for the entertainment of their young customers. One table cleaner, who dressed like a squirrel, found some holes in her squirrel costume in what she thought were rather embarrassing places, so she took the outfit to her supervisor to get it repaired. Instead of having the uniform fixed, he began teasing her about boy squirrels and girl squirrels, saying he thought that the holes were in "squirrel-appropriate locations." The final straw for the employee was when her supervisor came up behind her and pantomimed what a boy squirrel would do to a girl squirrel if she had a hole in that particular spot. The person who told me this story was the squirrel's attorney, at a party.

Again, I had those same doubting thoughts: the things people do to each other at work are a constant source of amazement, but an attorney! Had we gone too far again? Do we really need an attorney involved in a case like this?

A third story was about a young woman who went into her boss's office one afternoon to pick up an adding machine. Her boss was sitting at his desk, talking with a male employee who was standing across the desk from him. The woman walked around behind her boss's desk and bent over to pick up the machine. Her boss turned around in his swivel chair, to find her rump right in front of his face. The personnel director of this company told me that, without thinking, on the spur of the moment, with no malicious intent whatsoever, the boss "bit the woman on the butt."

If you're like most people, by now you're either shaking your head at these stories or smiling or laughing outright. But when people stop to think about harassment instead of just reacting, or when it happens to someone they're close to, like their wife or daughter, husband or son, then the situation changes.

Let's go back through those three stories, starting with the token clerk. If we assume that only twenty thousand people went through her work station on a daily basis and that only one of every hundred made some kind of sexual comment, that's two hundred comments in an eight-hour shift. Even if we assume that only one out of every two hundred made a comment, we're still talking about a hundred comments every single day. You can imagine how tired of that poster the woman was by noon of the first day, or how tired of it her husband was on the second evening, when he'd heard about nothing else for two days. The story's not quite so funny the second time around.

As for the table cleaner in the pizza parlor, it turns out that it wasn't she who had hired the attorney, but her mommy and daddy. The little squirrel was only fifteen years old, and her parents didn't think it was one bit funny when her twenty-two-year-old supervisor pantomimed boy squirrels and girl squirrels behind the counter at ten o'clock at night, when it was just the two of them alone in the store. Not so funny when you think it might be your daughter, granddaughter, or niece.

And the woman who was bitten didn't complain to anyone because she didn't want to get her boss in trouble; in fact, they were friends. But three weeks later she went to the human resources office and quit. When the personnel director tried to find out why she was leaving, she started crying and told him the story. It seems that the man who witnessed the biting went out and told everyone in the warehouse what he'd seen and how funny it was. Since then, people the woman didn't know had been coming up to her and teasing her about teeth marks or bruises on her behind; people would laugh and giggle when she walked into the lunchroom; some had even asked to see the "tattoo on [her] ass." So she wasn't going to cause problems for anyone. She was embarrassed and very uncomfortable, and she'd decided just to leave. This funny, stupid story just doesn't seem so funny after all, does it?

One early survey, published in 1981 in the *Harvard Business Review,* said that the real problem was not in defining sexual harassment but in recognizing it when it occurs. The results showed that men and women see sexual harassment very differently. Of course, now, with hindsight, that doesn't seem very surprising, but what it means is that if sexual harassment occurred right in front of us, many of the women would call it harassment and many of the men would call it a joke. And it's not even that simple, because opinions about what is and isn't harassment vary not just between men and women, but between men and men, and women and women.

Most often, people think of sexual harassment in two extremes. Many think that the only time it's sexual harassment is when a supervisor or manager says, "Sleep with me or you're fired." Of course that is sexual harassment—the most serious kind—but that is only the tip of the iceberg. At the other extreme are people who think or say that everything in the world is sexual harassment, and if you say "Hi, hon, how's it going?" that's sexual harassment and a suit could be filed against you. That's a slight exaggeration too.

We can think of sexual harassment in two different ways. First, there's what we call the behavioral definition: a common-sense, everyday way of looking at the problem. Second is what we'll call the legal definition: what the EEOC Guidelines and the courts define as illegal discrimination.

THE BEHAVIORAL OR COMMON-SENSE DEFINITION

The most common behavioral definition of sexual harassment is "deliberate and/or repeated sexual or sex-based behavior that is not welcome, not asked for, and not returned." There are three major elements and two qualifiers in this definition.

First of all, for it to be sexual harassment, *the behavior in question has to be sexual in nature or sex-based.* In other words, it's behavior with some sort of sexual connotation to it or behavior that occurs because of the victim's being male or female.

The range of behavior with sexual connotations is very wide, and the behavior doesn't necessarily mean that the perpetrator has the intent of having sex. We must think in terms of a continuum of sexual behavior, ranging from the least severe end— including joking, innuendoes, flirting, asking someone for a date—to the most serious end—forced fondling, attempted or actual rape, sexual assault.

As for sex-based behavior—occurring on account of sex or gender—it too can be light or severe. It is negative behavior that is directed at, or has an impact on, only one gender. Negative gender-related behavior can include men putting down the women or women making negative remarks about the men—in other words, a serious battle of the sexes at the job site.

One example I heard was the men saying to the women, "I can't believe your husband lets you work here," "This is man's work," "You should be home having babies," "You're here only because of the affirmative action program." These comments were not sexy or sexual, but were made because of gender or sex—the men didn't say this kind of thing to other men. When you see such a battle between the men and women, the more traditional type of sexual harassment is usually occurring too, or is not far behind. In terms of our first definition, you should consider this kind of behavior sexual harassment.

Second, *the behavior has to be deliberate and/or repeated.* Some forms of sexual behavior are so graphic and offensive that the first time they occur they are considered deliberate, inappropriate, and sometimes even illegal actions. There are other forms of behavior that must be repeated over and over again before they become harassment. Both are serious and damaging, but we tend to disagree over their being labeled "sexual harassment."

Most of us would agree that such severe sexual behavior as forced fondling, attempted rape, and serious sexual slurs definitely is not permissible. Where we have the difficulty and disagreement is at the other end of the continuum. What one person takes as joking another finds offensive and degrading.

Keep in mind that even comments made in a joking manner may not be bothersome the first few times, but day after day, joke after joke, they cease to be funny or amusing to the person who's receiving them. While the behavior may not be considered illegal sexual harassment, it still has a negative and damaging impact on the employee subjected to it.

One way of looking at it is to remember that *the more severe the behavior is, the fewer times it needs to be repeated before reasonable people define it as harassment; the less severe it is, the more times it needs to be repeated.* This is one of the two qualifiers of the definition. The severity of the behavior must be considered in conjunction with the number of repetitions.

The third part of the definition is that *sexual harassment is not welcome, not asked for, and not returned.* We are not talking about mutual behavior that people engage in together or enjoy. What two people do that is mutual is simply that, mutual, and is usually permissible so long as it doesn't interfere with their work or create a hostile or offensive work environment for others. (I say *usually* because some mutual behavior that may not be defined as harassment—because it *is* mutual—nevertheless still is not permissible in the work environment: mutual buttocks grabbing, mutual graphic sexual jokes, etc.)

When considering the welcomeness of the behavior, some people try to place the sole responsibility for setting limits on the victim: "It's not sexual harassment unless she or he says so." That's not quite right.

If we go back to the sexual-behavior continuum, we can add the second qualifier: *the less severe the behavior is, the more responsibility the receiver has to speak up* (because some people like this kind of behavior); *the more severe it is, the less responsibility the receiver has to speak up* (the initiator of the behavior should be sensitive enough in the first place to know that it is inappropriate).

The three elements—sexual or sex-based, deliberate and/or repeated, and not welcome, asked for, or returned—along with the two qualifiers of varying degrees of repetition and varying responsibilities of the sender and receiver, make up a complete, and some say too broad, definition of sexual harassment. It is primarily those with a legal perspective who initially feel that this definition may cover too much.

This definition covers more than what a purely legal definition might. The point is that studies have shown that light harassment tends to get worse and become severe when it is not addressed and stopped. By including in your assessment a definition of harassment that includes light, moderate, and severe, you can resolve the situation now and, it is to be hoped, in the future as well.

As for particular types of sexual harassment, it may be verbal, nonverbal, or physical. Verbal jokes, cracks, comments, and remarks are probably the most common form of harassment—what you're likely to see most often in complaints and investigations. Nonverbal harassment can be just as serious: certain kinds of looks, gestures, leering, ogling, photographs or cartoons. Physical harassment such as touching, pinching, rubbing, or "accidentally" brushing against someone's breasts or buttocks can be the

most severe form of harassment and can involve criminal charges.
It's also important to remember that sexual harassment is
really about power. The harasser either thinks or knows, consciously or unconsciously, that he or she has more power than the
harassee. If not, there would be no harassment—the harassee
could turn to the harasser and demand that it stop and there
would be no issue.

When asked why they file lawsuits or formal complaints outside their organizations—why they did not solve the problem
in-house—victims of harassment give two reasons:

- "I didn't think anyone would take me seriously." This says
  that they felt powerless. They thought or knew that others
  would laugh or tell them they were being too sensitive.
- "I couldn't get it stopped any other way." This indicates that
  they were powerless to stop unwanted behavior.

Deciding Whether Sexual Harassment Has Occurred

To determine whether behavior should be labeled sexual harassment, first compare it with the behavioral definition: deliberate
and/or repeated sexual or sex-based behavior that is not welcome,
not asked for, and not returned. Do this analysis for each incident
or act, then consider the overall picture.

1. Was the behavior sexual (about sex) or sex-based (on account of sex or directed to or affecting only one sex or gender)?
First, plot each occurrence on the continuum so you have some
picture of its severity:

- Potentially harassing behavior has the potential to be sexual
  harassment, particularly if repeated enough times, but it can
  also be socially acceptable in certain situations. This behavior
  is more likely to be called inappropriate or out of line, but not
  truly harassment, especially if just one instance has occurred.

- Subtle sexual behavior is sometimes socially acceptable, but some reasonable men and women would see it as offensive and want it stopped. The receivers usually don't want anything done to the sender at this point, other than making him or her stop. The behavior is bothersome, worth mentioning, but would not warrant a formal complaint if it were all that occurred.

- Moderate sexual behavior is not socially acceptable, and reasonable men and women see it as offensive and would want it stopped. The behavior is serious enough that some action must be taken against the sender (such as warning letters or reprimands), in addition to having him or her stop the behavior. The behavior is offensive and could warrant a complaint even if it were all that occurred.

- Severe sexual behavior is never socially acceptable and is so graphic or severe that one instance can call for serious disciplinary action, such as probation, suspension, or termination of the offending employee(s). Included in this category is physical behavior such as attempted or actual rape or sexual assault and verbal behavior such as serious sexual slurs.

2. Was the behavior deliberate and/or repeated? If it was not deliberate—truly accidental—then you mostly likely cannot label it harassment at all. If it was not accidental, then how often was it repeated? Remember the qualifier: the less severe the behavior, the more repetitions required to label it harassment; the more severe, the fewer repetitions needed. Also keep in mind that repeated instances of similar behavior can constitute repetitions: three different sexual remarks could be the same as three repetitions of one comment.

3. Was the behavior welcome, asked for, or returned? Again, remember the qualifier: the less severe the behavior, the more the

responsibility of the receiver to speak up; the more severe, the less responsibility the receiver has to speak up and the more responsibility the sender has to monitor his or her own behavior. Did the receiver tell or indicate to the sender that the behavior was unwelcome? Was it necessary that the receiver give notice, or should the sender have known better in the first place?

If the behavior was reciprocated in any way, was there a balance between the seriousness of the sender's behavior and the receiver's response? One of the arguments you will hear is that the complainant employee liked the behavior, engaged in it himself or herself, asked for it, encouraged it, etc. If this is the case, then both (or all) of the parties should be talked to so that this type of behavior is stopped (though it is not to be labeled sexual harassment, since it was welcome). However, first determine whether there was a balance between the sender's behavior and the receiver's response.

For example, if the alleged victim was telling off-color jokes in response to the alleged harasser's telling off-color jokes, then it would appear that the jokes were welcome and there was a balance in terms of severity of the conduct. But if the sender of the jokes used the receiver's telling of jokes as an invitation to go to a higher or more severe level—such as physical grabbing of buttocks or breasts—then the balance has shifted and the argument is not justified. Consider the balance in the severity of the behavior.

THE DEFINITION ACCORDING TO THE
EEOC GUIDELINES AND THE COURTS

The second step in determining whether sexual harassment has occurred is to consider each behavior, then the overall picture, in light of the EEOC Guidelines. There are several key points of the

Guidelines that need to be considered. These key points plus court decisions provide the legal definition of sexual harassment and spell out the rights and responsibilities of employers and employees. State laws may also pertain.

1. Section A of the Guidelines says that unwelcome sexual advances, requests for sexual favors, and other verbal or physical conduct of a sexual nature constitutes sexual harassment under any of four conditions:

- When such behavior is either explicitly or implicitly part of a manager's or supervisor's decision to hire or fire someone. When submitting to sexual conduct is a term or condition of employment, it is illegal, whether the request or demand was made outright or simply implied. Showing that such a request was implied might involve looking at employment records before and after the request was rejected. When an action amounts to the same thing as an explicit request, it too is illegal.

- When such behavior is used to make other employment decisions such as pay, promotion, or job assignment. Any time an employment decision is based on whether an employee submitted or refused to submit to some form of sexual conduct, it is illegal. The employment decision does not have to actually cost the employee his or her job, nor does the sexual conduct have to be an actual request for sex. The supervisor who plays favorites with workers who go along with his habit of telling dirty jokes or making sexual comments and bends the rules in their favor is making employment decisions based on willingness to submit to sexual conduct.

These two conditions are what courts have called quid pro quo harassment: someone with the power to do so, usually a supervisor or manager, offers some kind of tangible job benefit for submission to sexual harassment. In these cases courts have held the employer strictly liable—responsible even when the employer did not know the harassment was occurring and even if it had a policy forbidding such behavior.

- When such behavior has the purpose or effect of unreasonably interfering with the employee's work performance.
- When such behavior creates an intimidating, hostile, or offensive work environment.

Courts have called these two conditions hostile environment harassment: the damage caused by the sexual behavior does not have to be a tangible economic consequence such as losing the job or promotion, but the atmosphere at work becomes so negative that it affects the employee's ability to do his or her job. The sexual behavior is illegal harassment.

The EEOC included the words *purpose or effect* to indicate that intent to harm is not a necessary element of sexual harassment. If an employee's unwanted sexual behavior has the effect of creating a hostile work environment and interfering with another employee's work performance, the first employee's intent may be irrelevant.

To fit the EEOC's definition, sexual harassment must have two characteristics: it is unwelcome and unwanted and it has an impact on an employee's job or work environment. Whether the sexual behavior is directed to an employee face-to-face or behind his or her back, and whether the behavior occurs during breaks or in locker rooms, may not be important so long as it has an impact on the employee's work environment.

2. Section B says that each claim of sexual harassment should be examined on a case-by-case basis. Consideration should be given to the context in which the behavior took place, the nature

of the sexual behavior, and the record as a whole.

3. Sections C and D have to do with the employer's liability. Section C says that the employer may be held "strictly liable" for harassment by supervisors—meaning even when the employer is not aware of the harassment and even when there is a policy forbidding such behavior. Section D says that the employer is liable for co-worker harassment when the employer knows of the harassment and fails to take immediate and appropriate action.

Several courts ruled in 1983 that "strict liability" applies only in quid pro quo harassment cases, in which a tangible job benefit was affected, and the victim can file a charge without notifying management of the harassment. If it is hostile environment harassment, the victim must allow the employer the opportunity to take appropriate action before the victim can file a complaint. This issue is still being addressed by the courts.

4. Section E says that the employer may be held responsible for sexual harassment of its employees by people who are nonemployees—such as customers or the general public—when the employer knows about the harassment and does nothing. In these cases the extent of the employer's control over the situation is examined closely, and if in any way the employer can stop the harassment, it is responsible for doing so.

5. Section F says that employers should take all necessary steps to prevent sexual harassment from occurring in the first place. This includes policy statements, training for employees, and grievance procedures.

6. Section G says that if one employee submits to sexual requests and gains benefits thereby, other employees, equally well qualified, may sue on the basis of sex discrimination for not being allowed those same benefits or opportunities. If a supervisor gives the best job assignments to a subordinate because of their sexual activities, other employees, both male and female, could claim

sex discrimination because they were denied those job assignments. This section of the Guidelines was upheld by a federal court in Delaware.

But the question, what does the law say, is just like the other questions—it has no simple answer either. What "the law" says can be interpreted to mean what the EEOC Guidelines say, what the 1964 Civil Rights Act says, what the courts are saying, or a combination of all three. A good basic answer is to think in these terms—for behavior to be considered illegal sexual harassment, it must meet these criteria:

- It occurs because of the person's sex—it is related to or about sex.
- It is unwelcome, not returned, not mutual.
- It affects the terms or conditions of employment, including the work environment itself.

CHAPTER SUMMARY

The most widely used, common-sense definition of sexual harassment is "deliberate and/or repeated sexual or sex-based behavior that is not welcome, not asked for, and not returned."

The less severe behavior is, the more times it must be repeated before it is considered sexual harassment.

The more severe behavior is, the fewer times it must be repeated before it is considered sexual harassment.

The less severe behavior is, the more responsibility the receiver has to speak up and make it known that it is offensive or unwelcome.

The more severe behavior is, the less responsibility the receiver has to speak up, and the more responsibility the perpetrator of the behavior has to know better than to engage in that behavior in the first place.

The EEOC Guidelines state that unwanted sexual advances, requests for sexual favors, and other verbal or physical actions of a sexual nature become illegal when connected to a manager's or supervisor's decision regarding hiring, firing, pay, promotion, job assignment, or other aspect of employment, or when such sexual behavior interferes with an employee's ability to perform work or creates a hostile, offensive work environment.

3

Six Simple Steps to Stop Sexual Harassment

The punch line to the joke was when he grabbed her crotch. And when he delivered the punch line, she lost control. She got hysterical and started crying and sobbing, and nobody could get her to stop. They finally had to call her husband to come to work and try to calm her down. When they told him what had happened, he didn't think the joke was very funny either.

This case ended up in court. The grabber was a leadman, a first-level supervisor, and the woman was a journeyman electrician. The jury awarded the woman $265,000 for the two years of harassment she had endured, even though she and her attorney had hoped to win only around $100,000. Two of the young men on the jury were so angry that they wanted to give her a million dollars.

The problems the company had in understanding and dealing with sexual harassment had become more and more apparent during the trial. It looked as if they had made only a halfhearted attempt to do anything at all about the harassment that they knew was taking place. The jury believed the woman's allegation—that her employer was liable because it failed to maintain a work environment free of sexually harassing conduct and comments, and to that extent the environment was unsafe and hostile toward women.

The testimony given indicated that management did not take a strong stance against harassment, that its policy statement and procedures for handling complaints were weak, that sexual harassment training was insufficient and ineffectual, and that little or no follow-up was done on specific complaints or on the sexual harassment problem in general. This case was a perfect example of what a company should not do.

Those companies and organizations that successfully stop or prevent sexual harassment in their workplaces have comprehensive programs in place that include six primary elements. When you see a serious sexual harassment complaint, like the one described above, you can be fairly certain that one or more of these elements is missing: (1) top management support, (2) a written, posted policy statement, (3) procedures for getting and handling complaints, (4) actual handling of complaints, (5) training for all employees, and (6) follow-through.

MANAGEMENT SUPPORT

Any qualified, knowledgeable organizational consultant will tell you that the atmosphere (or, in new terms, the "culture") of an organization comes down from the top. This atmosphere is revealed in written and spoken terms and in unspoken terms too—the everyday behavior demonstrated by those at the top. Everyone knows that the adage "Actions speak louder than words" is basically true. The attitude taken and displayed by the leaders of the organization must be that *sexual harassment is a serious problem that interferes with productivity,* and that *it is a business and legal issue.* The fact that it is also a social or women's issue is of secondary concern in the business context. This attitude of seriousness, initially exhibited by top management, will be passed down and throughout the entire organization. While not everyone will accept or share this perception of the problem, it affects the way the problem is approached.

The best approach will be positive and oriented toward problem solving. Sexual harassment is perceived as an on-the-job problem to be addressed and solved, just like any other issue affecting the overall organization. The successful companies' programs are direct and not overly threatening, and they include everyone—employees at all levels.

However, consider this: a 1988 survey by *Working Woman* magazine showed that nearly 90 percent of the Fortune 500 companies responding had had complaints of sexual harassment in the previous year; more than 33 percent had been sued once, and nearly 25 percent had been sued repeatedly. Yet 40 percent of the companies had provided no sexual harassment training at all, and 42 percent provided training to managers only.

Obviously, top management's attitude toward sexual harassment can be an obstacle to both adoption and effectiveness of a comprehensive program. Equally important is the fact that management's attitude—refusing to acknowledge, overlooking, trivializing—can actually contribute to sexual harassment problems. Because of management's nonsupport, there may be more instances of harassment, more-severe harassment, or complaints that have been ignored for so long that the situation is much worse than it would have been otherwise.

The *Working Woman* report states, "Commitment from the top makes a difference. When senior management is perceived as making the prevention of sexual harassment a top priority, firms are far more likely to offer training programs and to establish mechanisms to encourage the reporting of both formal and informal complaints."

POLICY STATEMENT

A written, posted policy statement regarding sexual harassment follows logically from top management support. It must be written and it must be posted; a verbal policy is in actuality no policy at all, and an unposted policy is not only difficult to read but sometimes impossible to find. One company that assured me it had a policy was still searching for it three weeks after I asked to see it.

Actually, there are a number of ways in which the policy can be distributed or made known to employees. The *Working Woman* survey showed that the companies responding make use of a variety of ways: include it in the employee handbook (54 percent), post it on bulletin boards (51 percent), distribute it during workshops or seminars on the topic (51 percent), and/or include it in orientation materials for new employees (44 percent). However, of the 44 percent that include it in orientation materials, only 27 percent discuss it with new managers, and only 19 percent discuss it with new employees.

The policy should explicitly address sexual harassment and should be more specific than a general antiharassment or nondiscrimination policy. A good policy has at least four effects, in that it will:

- Demonstrate management's understanding of the issue and its commitment to eliminating the problem.
- Establish and make known the procedures for handling instances of sexual harassment.

- Begin to educate employees about the problem of sexual harassment.
- Encourage employees to come forward with their complaints.

A policy should include these elements:

1. Purpose of the policy
2. Legal definition of sexual harassment
3. Behavioral definition of sexual harassment
4. Importance of the problem
5. How employees should handle harassment
6. How the organization handles incidents or complaints
7. Disciplinary action
8. Names and phone numbers of individuals to call

SAMPLE POLICY STATEMENT

1. *Purpose:* This policy is intended to set forth this organization's position as it relates to sexual harassment.

2. *Legal Definition:* Sexual harassment is a form of sex discrimination and is an "unlawful employment practice" under Title VII of the 1964 Civil Rights Act. Unwelcome sexual advances, requests for sexual favors, and other verbal or physical conduct constitute sexual harassment when:

   - They are part of a manager's or supervisor's decision to hire or fire.
   - They are used to make other employment decisions such as pay, promotion, or job assignment.
   - They interfere with the employee's work performance.
   - They create an intimidating, hostile, or offensive work environment.

3. *Behavior That Can Constitute Sexual Harassment:* Sexual harassment is defined as deliberate or repeated behavior of a sexual nature which is unwelcome. It can include verbal behavior

such as unwanted sexual comments, suggestions, jokes, or pressure for sexual favors; nonverbal behavior such as suggestive looks or leering; and physical behavior such as pats or squeezes, or repeatedly brushing against someone's body.

Some specific examples of inappropriate or illegal behavior include:

- Negative or offensive comments, jokes, or suggestions about another employee's gender or sexuality.
- Obscene or lewd sexual comments, jokes, suggestions, or innuendoes.
- Slang, names, or labels, such as "honey," "sweetie," "boy," "girl," that others find offensive.
- Talking about or calling attention to an employee's body or sexual characteristics in a negative or embarrassing way.
- Laughing at, ignoring, or not taking seriously an employee who experiences sexual harassment.
- Blaming the victims of sexual harassment for causing the problems.
- Continuing certain behavior after a co-worker has objected to that behavior.
- Displaying nude or sexual pictures, cartoons, or calendars on company or organization property.

4. *Importance of the Problem:* Sexual harassment negatively affects morale, motivation, and job performance. It results in increased absenteeism, turnover, inefficiency, and loss of productivity. It is inappropriate, offensive, and illegal, and it will not be tolerated in this organization.

5. *Employee Procedure:* This organization will take an affirmative role in protecting its employees from sexual harassment. Should an instance of inappropriate behavior occur, it is the employee's responsibility to bring it to the attention of management. This includes employees who think that they are the recipient of sexual harassment and also those who believe that they have witnessed another employee's being harassed.

If you believe you are being sexually harassed, take action immediately by:

- Identifying the offensive behavior to the harasser and requesting that it stop.
- Discussing your concern immediately with a supervisor, manager, personnel official, or other employee authorized to deal with discrimination complaints, such as the EEO counselor or affirmative action representative.

6. *Organizational Procedures:* When a supervisor or manager is notified of alleged harassment, he or she will promptly investigate the complaint. The investigation may include interviews with the directly involved parties and, where necessary, with employees who may have observed the alleged harassment or who may be similarly situated with the complaining employee and may be able to testify to his or her experiences with the accused employee.

7. *Disciplinary Action:* Complaints and cases of sexual harassment will be dealt with promptly. An employee who sexually harasses another employee will be disciplined as in any other case of serious, illegal employee misconduct.
If the investigation shows that the accused employee did engage in harassment, the supervisor will take appropriate action, which will include a warning that any continued harassment may result in a negative employment action, such as suspension or termination. Additional actions that may be taken include verbal and/or written reprimands, a letter in the employee's file, or an employee transfer, where warranted.

8. *Questions or Concerns:* It is our intention to make this organization an enjoyable place to work for all employees, and we will actively seek to identify areas of concern and take appropriate action.

An employee who has questions or concerns regarding this policy should talk with his or her supervisor or _____ [name and title of the person authorized to deal with discrimination matters] at _____ [phone number].

According to *Working Woman,* a good sexual harassment policy needs to "convey consistent messages" that:

> Sexual harassment will not be tolerated—its presence is damaging to all employees and to the organizational climate;
>
> Complainants will be protected from reprisal; employees are encouraged to come forward confidentially to discuss situations which make them uncomfortable and to learn about their options;
>
> Those found guilty of harassment will be disciplined consistently with others who have violated workplace policies, and without regard to their position or job performance.

PROCEDURES FOR GETTING AND HANDLING COMPLAINTS

The purpose of complaint procedures is simply to provide the means for getting complaints out into the open—a way to bring problems to the attention of those who can help solve them—and to resolve the problems. Effective procedures will allow organizations the opportunity to handle problems themselves, before complaints are made to an external agency.

Because of the nature of sexual harassment problems, these complaint procedures should be flexible, and offer more than one route for employees to complain or to get information about their concerns. The procedures should be designed and communicated so that employees realize that complaints and questions are welcomed and not discouraged.

It's a good idea for the sexual harassment complaint procedure to be different from other complaint or "always use the chain-of-command" type of procedures in the organization. The usual practice of having the supervisor as the first contact can present and create even more problems. In many cases the supervisor is either the actual or alleged harasser or a friend of the actual or alleged harasser. Studies have shown that the supervisor is often perceived as a weak link in the sexual harassment complaint procedure.

It's best to simply allow people the option of going around or above the supervisor. This practice will upset some supervisors, but the goal is to get complaints out in the open, where they can be effectively resolved—regardless of whom the complaint is made to. I sometimes ask supervisors in my workshops which they'd prefer—to have their own supervisor come knocking on the door because one of their subordinates has gone over their head with a complaint of sexual harassment, or to have the subordinate's attorney come knocking on the door. Obviously, the point is that we want to get complaints made, investigated, and resolved in-house whenever possible.

Allow employees the option of complaining to the supervisor or to any of several other designated individuals, with no particular order assigned. The designated people need to be perceived as credible, objective, and sensitive to the problem of sexual harassment, and it helps to have one of them be a woman.

The complaint procedures don't need to be complicated and can usually be included as part of the policy statement. An example from the Washington State Human Rights Commission:

> Any employee who believes he or she is being harassed by co-workers or customers should notify his or her supervisor. Where the employee believes that he or she is being harassed by his/her supervisor, he/she should notify the supervisor's supervisor. Where the employee is uncomfortable in discussing harassment with his/her supervisor, the personnel department may be contacted instead of the supervisor. No

employee will be retaliated against in any way for complaining of harassment.

Allowing the complaining employee to remain anonymous is not a necessary element of the procedure. It may or may not be appropriate, depending on the situation. The rights of all parties must be protected, and in many cases the accused ultimately has a right to know the accuser. Never promise complaining employees that you'll keep what they say confidential. It's a promise you sometimes can't keep.

It's also not necessary that the complaint always be in writing or that it be signed. Simply write down the complaint and specific allegations and use those notes in resolving the situation. It is a good idea to read what you've noted as the complaint and allegations back to the complaining employee to make sure you have it correct. If the complaint is in writing, fine; if not, proceed anyway. I've actually seen managers refuse to conduct an investigation because the complaining employee would not put the allegations in writing. Once you have knowledge of the allegations or behavior, you can go ahead to resolve the problem.

HANDLING COMPLAINTS

How complaints have been handled in the past sends a message to the people in the organization about how the organization perceives sexual harassment and the value it places on its employees. It sets a tone, either positive or negative, that affects future occurrences and complaints of harassment. To know the impact past complaints have had on your organization, you need to know a bit about what has happened before. As much as possible, see if you can find some answers to the following:

Were past complaints handled quickly, in a timely fashion, so that the people involved knew they were being taken seriously and handled with care?

Was enough time spent on complaints, or were they just rushed through? On the other hand, was too much time spent, so that the people involved felt overburdened for a long period of time?

Do past investigations appear to have been fair to all parties involved? Do the people involved think that past investigations were fair?

In the end, did past investigations result in actions that took care of all necessary parts: the situation (was the harassment stopped); the alleged harasser (was discipline, if necessary, appropriate, i.e., did the punishment fit the crime); the alleged victim (was he or she provided appropriate remedies and options in addition to having the harassment stopped); and the rest of the work group (were they informed as much as possible about the result; did anyone take responsibility for healing this work group)?

Were the past resulting actions directed only at the specific complaint or at the overall problem (management support, policy, procedures, etc.) or both?

For example, if you know that past complaints were mishandled, from either lack of concern or lack of knowledge, you can make an extra effort to address those errors in future complaints. If you know that people felt that a past investigation was rushed, you can make sure to schedule more than enough time for interviews in future complaints and let people know from the beginning that plenty of time is available to them. If you know (or believe or are concerned) that employees felt left out or uninformed at the end of a past investigation because no one ever got back to them for any sort of closure, you can make sure that closure will be part of future complaint resolutions and let people know how and when you'll get back to them at the end.

See the point? When beginning to work on a complaint, you may initially think that it is a very narrow or well-defined problem you are addressing. I've not found this to be the case. To the contrary: you are not only going into a particular situation that has its own history (sexual harassment usually involves an ongoing, repetitive pattern of behavior) but also into an organization, department, or work group that also has a history around this issue. The more you know about what happened in the past, about attitudes, values, and opinions, the better for you and for the effective resolution of complaints. For more details, see Chapter 4 or my book *Sexual Harassment: Investigator's Manual* (1991).

TRAINING PROGRAMS

When working in the area of sexual harassment, two somewhat contradictory questions come up over and over again: (1) Don't you think most people know what sexual harassment is? and (2) Don't you think this sexual harassment issue is getting even grayer and more difficult to define?

The answer to both those questions is "no." Most people don't know what sexual harassment is, and because it has the word *sex* in it and because they do know that it's against the law, they're afraid to ask. And no, the issue is not getting fuzzier; it's actually becoming clearer and easier to understand.

The real problem is that people are not educated about what sexual harassment is, what it costs, and what they should or shouldn't do. Once they are provided some training (and it can be as little as two to three hours), most people understand, and in fact agree, that it is a serious problem and they'll try to help stop it (or at least won't do it themselves). Meanwhile, companies continue to hold their employees responsible for living up to standards about sexual harassment when those employees don't even know about the standards, much less understand them.

From data generated in the *Working Woman* study cited earlier, one estimate is that nearly 82 percent of the companies responding need immediate help in training their employees— either with a first-time training effort or with additional effort to train supervisors and general employees. The survey showed that harassment can cost the typical Fortune 500 service or manufacturing company $6.7 million per year in absenteeism, turnover, and lost productivity associated with sexual harassment, at a cost of $282.53 per employee. These figures do not include the costs of litigation, responding to charges filed with regulatory agencies, destructive behavior, or sabotage. On the other hand, the survey said that meaningful steps—such as employee training—can be undertaken for as little as $200,000, or $8.41 per employee. It is nearly "34 times [as] expensive to ignore the problem."

A sound training program should consist of a series of presentations and workshops for all employees, divided into separate sessions for three levels: top, executive-level management, supervisors and other managers, and general-level employees. The emphasis should be on behavioral changes on the job, and secondly on attitudinal changes. *Changes in attitude are beneficial but optional; changes in behavior are required.*

The trainer or instructor should use teaching techniques, such as lecture, presentation, discussion, question-and-answer, case studies, or exercises, that are most appropriate to each group; each session should be tailored to the trainees' needs. The topic of sexual harassment should be presented as a work-related and productivity issue rather than as a social or moral issue, and it should emphasize the costs to all employees and to the work environment.

Each and every employee should be included at some time in a training or educational effort. To be most effective, the training should be part of the larger, overall effort including the policy statement, disciplinary action, and management support.

Whether your company has provided employee training on sexual harassment will have a significant impact on complaints and their resolution. Sometimes the accused will say they didn't know they were harassing anyone; supervisors will sometimes say they weren't notified or didn't know that the harassment was occurring; victims will say they didn't complain because they didn't know if they should or how to go about it. Effective training can eliminate these reasons in the first place. For more details about training, see Chapter 5 or my book *Sexual Harassment: Training Manual* (1988).

FOLLOW UP AND FOLLOW THROUGH

This simply means to use your head, to think, and to use a little common sense to make sure that all loose ends are tied up. A small but sometimes costly mistake that many companies make is to assume that once they've "done" their sexual harassment program, it's over, finished, complete. That's almost true, but not quite.

Remember to take care of what seem to be small details at the end. Make sure that employee training occurs on an annual basis, for new employees as part of employee orientation (even if it's just two or three employees at a time); provide supervisors, especially those newly promoted to supervisory positions, with updates and reminders in the form of annual training; and if problems arise, resolve them quickly and fairly, and use each case as an opportunity to reaffirm management's position that such behavior—sexual harassment—will not be tolerated at your company.

CHAPTER SUMMARY

Management's negative attitude about the problem—refusing to acknowledge, overlooking, or trivializing sexual harassment—can actually contribute to sexual harassment problems.

The attitude taken and displayed by management must be that sexual harassment is a serious problem that interferes with productivity, that it is bad for business, and that it's against the law.

A written, posted policy that explicitly addresses sexual harassment is critical and follows from management support.

Procedures for getting and handling complaints are to provide the means for getting complaints out in the open. Procedures should be flexible, offering employees more than one route to complain or get information.

Complaints should be handled quickly, thoroughly, and in a way that is fair to all parties and takes care of all those involved in the situation.

Training and education are effective tools in stopping and preventing sexual harassment. Training about this problem should be provided to each and every employee.

Efforts at eliminating sexual harassment should be seen as an overall, ongoing program within the company or organization, not as just a one-time or short-term issue.

4

How to Handle Sexual Harassment Complaints

The most difficult complaint I ever dealt with started with one woman who said she was being sexually harassed by her co-worker, a security guard. She said she didn't want anything done to him, she just wanted him to stop. The company decided to examine the problem more closely and asked me to do a full investigation. He denied everything, but after interviewing close to thirty people I found at least nine women who had been sexually harassed over a period of years by this man. He was terminated immediately.

This kind of situation involves what is called a complex complaint: one in which an actual in-depth investigation must be done. The problem cannot be resolved between the two employees alone, so other employees must be interviewed. Investigations can take a good deal of time, energy, and expertise, and are usually handled by the human resources department or an outside investigator.

On the other hand, the easiest complaint I ever dealt with was when a woman complained and told me what the man had done, and the man admitted he had done it but said he hadn't meant it the way she took it. The three of us sat down together; they talked, resolved their differences, and agreed to go forward. That's what anyone would call a simple complaint.

This kind of situation—a simple complaint—is when the only people involved are the complaining employee and the alleged harasser. The problem can usually be handled by a supervisor or manager's talking with only the two employees and resolving it. This is not to say that the complaint is trivial or not severe—it could involve a very serious infraction such as physical harassment. However, the problem is resolved by the supervisor/manager's talking with only the alleged victim and the alleged harasser, and then taking appropriate action. In other words, no true investigative work is necessary.

HANDLING SIMPLE COMPLAINTS

This section is to help supervisors, managers, human resources professionals, and others responsible for resolution of such problems in handling simple sexual harassment complaints, though many of the points can also apply to in-depth investigations. Handling complaints involves four primary elements: interviews with the complainant, the alleged harasser, and any witnesses; an assessment of the incident by the supervisor or manager; a review of available records; and appropriate action.

Interviews

In the initial interview with the complaining employee, the supervisor (or manager) should make it clear that he or she is sympathetic to the employee's complaint, that confidentiality will be maintained as much as possible, and that a true, accurate, and complete account of the incident(s) is needed.

The supervisor should determine the facts upon which the employee's complaint is based. This means finding, as specifically as possible, the who, what, when, and where elements of the complaint. The employee should be asked to provide available evidence, including the names of other individuals who can corroborate the incident or have experienced similar behavior.

The initial interview should end with the supervisor asking the complaining employee what action the company could take to resolve the incident satisfactorily. It is appropriate for the supervisor to suggest several possible solutions to the problem. These informal solutions might include an apology from the offender or a meeting with the two employees and the supervisor together. The supervisor should tell the employee that this does not mean that the company will necessarily do what the employee asks; at this point, options are simply being explored.

It is not appropriate for the supervisor to follow the suggestion of the employee to "just let it go this time" in the hope that the behavior will not happen again, unless the infraction is minor and/or accidental. In that case, the supervisor should follow up on a regular basis to make sure the behavior has ceased.

The second interview, with the alleged harasser, should inform the employee that a complaint has been made against him or her. To the extent possible, the name of the complainant should not be revealed. If the person's identity is known, it should be made clear to the alleged harasser that no retaliatory action will be tolerated. The accused employee should also be told not to discuss this matter either with co-workers or with the alleged victim.

Since many times the employee will deny the allegations, the supervisor should try to corroborate minor facts and get the other side of the story. At this point the supervisor may have to begin to make credibility judgments. If the employee agrees that the incident took place, the supervisor may again suggest informal remedies and proceed with them. If the employee totally denies or disagrees with the allegations of the complainant, he or she should be told that further interviews with witnesses will be conducted. (At this point, if a third round of interviews is to begin with witnesses identified by both alleged harasser and victim, the process has moved from one of simple complaint resolution to a complex complaint investigation. A complex investigation requires additional steps. For information, see *Sexual Harassment: Investigator's Manual.*)

Interviews with employees is only one aspect of the complaint resolution process. The other factors listed below should also be considered in examining the complaint.

Assessing the Incident

Both the EEOC Guidelines and case law suggest that each instance of harassment should be examined on a case-by-case basis and the "totality of the circumstances" considered. Both the behavioral, common-sense definition of harassment and the EEOC's definition of harassment should be used to examine the complaint.

It is often claimed that sexual harassment is all "subjective" and all "depends on the victim's perceptions." Of course, to some extent this is true, for what is harassing to one person may not be to another; there are no lists of right and wrong behavior.

However, Patricia Linenberger, in *Labor Law Journal* (November 1981), listed factors based on the premise that the identification of sexual harassment can be made as a result of an objective assessment. She says the question to be asked is "how would the reasonable person in the same or similar circumstances perceive the conduct?" and that the perception of the victim and the intent of the harasser should be irrelevant. Some of the factors we've already covered, but some are new. Regardless, a second look is worth the time for you in your analysis:

- Severity of the conduct: Generally, behavior can be placed along a continuum ranging from mild to severe. While no hard lines can be drawn, general groupings can be made.
- Number and frequency of encounters: The number of incidents and the time span between them is important. What seems less severe when happening only once may become more serious when repeated often and with persistence.
- Apparent intent of the harasser: The question to be asked is what reasonable people would have meant had they acted in a similar manner. Also important is whether the behavior was directed at the victim or simply overheard or seen.
- Relationship of the two employees: Studies reveal that people generally expect higher levels of conduct from supervisors. What may be permissible from a co-worker is inappropriate from supervisory personnel and may be more serious and more threatening because of the power relationship. Also to be considered is the nature of their interpersonal relationship—do they generally get along well, have they had an ongoing feud for some time, were they involved romantically?
- Victim's provocation: The behavior of the victim should be considered but not overweighted. Blaming the victim for causing the harassment is a common pattern that should be avoided. However, if the receiving employee does provoke or elicit such behavior, then it loses its "unwelcome" connotation.
- Response of the victim: It is generally assumed that the victim has some responsibility for communicating that behavior is unwelcome. This responsibility makes more sense when considered in light of the severity of the conduct di-

rected toward him or her. The more severe the conduct, such as forced fondling or attempted rape, the less responsibility the victim has to express objection. The milder the conduct, such as jokes or teasing, the more responsibility the victim has to speak up. This factor should be weighted, since many victims are afraid to respond honestly, especially when the offending employee is a supervisor or a well-liked co-worker.

- Effect on the victim: An assessment should be made of the consequences of the offensive behavior to the employee and the seriousness of the injury. Was the employee embarrassed, humiliated, physically injured, demoted, denied a promotion?
- Work environment: Reasonable people usually expect different behavior depending on the nature of the work environment. What is appropriate in a blue-collar factory may not be appreciated or appropriate in a white-collar office.
- Public or private situations: Different types of harassing behavior could be more or less serious depending on whether they happened publicly or privately.
- Men–women ratio: Studies have shown that the higher the ratio of men to women in the work environment, the more likely sexual harassment is to occur.

Each of these factors must be considered in its relationship to the others. Various factors should be given different weight depending on the particular situation. In some situations, such as physical sexual abuse, only one factor may be relevant. In this instance, the behavior is so severe that the other nine factors are of little relevance. However, with verbal or visual harassment, all ten factors may be required to make an objective assessment.

Once the interviews are completed and the incident is assessed, the supervisor should proceed to the next step.

Review of Records

A review of available personnel records is pertinent, particularly when the accusation involves a supervisor. It's essential to determine whether a history of friction exists between the two. The employee's records should be reviewed with regard to supervisory ratings, performance reviews, promotions or pass-overs for promotions, transfers, raises, and disciplinary actions. The supervisor's records should be reviewed to ascertain problems with other employees, previous allegations of misconduct, or other factors that would tend to verify the employee's claim.

When the complaint involves two co-workers, a review of their records may indicate a prior problem between them, accusations of the same nature by other employees, or previous problems with the alleged victim that would tend to invalidate the claim.

Taking Appropriate Action

If the two employees generally agree during their separate interviews that the incident(s) did occur, bringing the two of them together to discuss the issue can sometimes prove very effective in resolving the problem. This is especially useful when misunderstandings or different interpretations of behavior have taken place. For example, the male co-worker who continually asks a female employee out for a date feels he is breaking down her resistance. She feels harassed and perhaps intimidated. Differences in perception, communication, and values are the issues that call for clarification.

In more serious cases the above approach can simply harden attitudes between the two parties. If the harassment was severe and blatant, the victim may feel too embarrassed or demeaned to confront the harasser. Once the information is corroborated, *it is ultimately the employer's responsibility to deal with the harassing employee.*

The disciplinary action that should be taken should be based on an analysis of the ten factors listed under "Assessing the Incident" and the two definitions of harassment, the behavioral definition and the EEOC's definition, in Chapter 2. The level of discipline can be categorized as mild, moderate, or severe.

Mild discipline would include a discussion with the offending employee about the behavior, indicating that such behavior must be stopped. This could be followed by a letter or memo from the employer to the offending employee stressing company policy against sexual harassment. No record of the complaint is included in the employee's file; however, the employer should maintain a record of the actions taken during and as a result of the investigation.

Moderate discipline would include a meeting with the offending employee plus a written warning or disciplinary notice in his or her file. The warning should indicate action to be taken should further offenses occur or removal of the notice if no further offense takes place within a specified time.

Severe discipline would include suspension, probation, demotion, transfer, or termination of the offending employee. If the harassment has caused the victim some tangible damage, such as a poor personnel record, denial of a promotion, poor performance reviews, etc., this situation should be rectified before the complaint is considered complete.

In general, discipline for sexual harassment should follow progressive disciplinary procedures: with each infraction of the rules, the punishment meted out is more severe. The number of infractions must, of course, be balanced against the severity of each offense, as determined by assessing the incident(s). One serious offense calls for severe discipline; minor offenses, when repeated a number of times, may require the same severe discipline.

The individual handling the complaint should continue to stay in contact with the work group for a reasonable time after settling the harassment issue, to ensure that the situation remains satisfactory. Periodic and regular follow-up, particularly with the victim, makes sure that harassing behavior has been stopped, that retaliation is not occurring, and that the employees are working together productively, effectively, and in a professional manner.

After a harassment complaint, it often takes some time for the interpersonal relationships among all the employees to return to normal, especially between accused and accuser. Staying in close communication with the work group during this time will benefit everyone.

One of the most difficult decisions arises when the case or complaint is inconclusive. Failing to take action against the offending employee can expose the organization to substantial liability, especially in the case of an offending supervisor. On the other hand, imposing discipline on the employee without sufficient cause is unfair, creates morale problems, and can also expose the company to liability.

True cases of one employee's word against another are rare. With few exceptions, a thorough investigation will reveal witnesses to the same or similar behavior on the part of the accused, or identify other victims. The supervisor handling the complaint should be careful to not assume innocence on the part of the alleged harasser simply because the complaint cannot be substantiated.

In inconclusive cases, the company should warn the accused employee that it considers the allegations serious, and that although the facts are disputed, such conduct is forbidden and will not be tolerated. The complaint should be fully documented so that any future occurrences can be assessed in the appropriate context. It is sometimes advisable to place memos in both employees' files reflecting the inconclusive nature of the complaint.

The files can be purged after a period of time with no further incidents.

In rare cases the alleged victim's complaint will turn out to be fictitious or even malicious. Such a complaint does not involve a misunderstanding or differing interpretations of the situation, as mentioned previously, but a false complaint filed with the intent to retaliate against or harm the alleged harasser. When the untrue nature of the charge is substantiated, the alleged victim should be disciplined for filing a false complaint.

Individuals handling complaints should be careful of the "frivolous" complaint. First of all, such complaints are the exception and rare. Second, the impact of disciplining an alleged victim of harassment can have a considerable effect on whether future legitimate complaints are made. Obviously, letting an employee "get away with" filing malicious charges damages morale as well. Be certain the complaint is false before disciplining complainants.

ABOUT VICTIMS AND HARASSERS

About Victims

Since the issue of sexual harassment has been brought to public attention, data regarding harassers and harassed have been accumulating. Often people want to know what "typical" victims or harassers are like, or they ask for a "profile." While such information is now available, though still somewhat sketchy, certain dangers exist when describing the typical case.

Once the general behavior or characteristics of victims of harassment have been identified, it becomes too easy for some people to begin to expect or look for those kinds of actions from victims. With that perception or frame of reference, the next logical assumption is that the victims have control: if they didn't act or look in certain ways, they wouldn't be harassed. From there, the pattern of blaming the victim is apparent: something about the person actually causes him or her to be harassed or victimized.

Keeping in mind this problem, certain very general statements can be made about people who are victims of sexual harassment:

- Most victims are female. Estimates are that approximately 90 percent of incident reports are made by women.
- Female victims are younger than the general female population. The women are usually in their twenties or thirties, specifically twenty-four to thirty-four for more severe forms of harassment.
- Women who are married or widowed are less likely to be harassed than women who are divorced, separated, or never married.
- While one study showed that 51 percent of the female victims were trainees and 47 percent earned an annual income of less than $10,999, generally women who are well educated are as likely to be harassed as less-educated women.
- Male victims of harassment are much more likely than female victims to be subjected to homosexual harassment. One study showed that 22 percent of the men who had been harassed said it had been done by a man or men; only 3 percent of the women said they had been bothered by another woman.
- Male victims are generally older than their female harassers.

Like all profiles, this is just an outline of who is most likely to be harassed. Not mentioned are the women and men who don't fit the pattern. Several studies have shown that victims are to be found in all age groups, marital statuses, job categories, pay ranges, and racial and ethnic groups.

Male or female, people experiencing sexual harassment report feeling angry, upset, frightened, guilty, embarrassed, demeaned, intimidated, or violated. Stress-related physical symptoms are headaches, backaches, and stomach problems. Effects also include feelings of being trapped, powerless, or defeated; loss of ambition; decreased job satisfaction; and impairment of job performance. One woman from the *Harvard Business Review* study wrote, "Sexual harassment eats away at the core of a woman's being, destroys self-confidence, and contributes to a lowered feeling of self-worth." Interviews have indicated that the feelings are similar for both male and female victims of harassment.

About Harassers

Obviously, the same risks of stereotyping exist when describing harassers as when describing victims. However, the studies do reveal a somewhat clearer picture of people who are guilty of sexual harassment.

- Usually harassers are male and older than their victims, married, and considered unattractive by the victims.
- Numerically, most harassers are co-workers, if for no other reason than the fact that most employees are nonsupervisory, but the most severe and most frequently reported harassment is from supervisors to subordinates.
- Harassers frequently bother more than one person, and the incidents reoccur over an extended period of time.
- The higher the percentage of men in the work group, the more harassment of women occurs.
- Motives for sexual harassment by men fall into three categories: actual sexual desire, personal power (by harassment the man makes himself feel more important, virile, etc.), and social control (the man who does not want women in the work

environment harasses to get rid of them or to "put them in their place").

- Most men do not sexually harass. One estimate is that only 5 percent of men are even capable of such behavior.
- Female harassers are involved in an estimated 1 percent of cases. Their victims are almost always men; homosexual female harassment is rare.
- Female harassers are usually divorced or single and younger than their victims.
- The "average" man who propositions or harasses a woman is much like the "average" man in the work force. The "average" woman who makes advances is not at all typical of the "average" working woman: she may be young, and is likely to be a supervisor.

Responses of Victims

In cases of sexual harassment, both victims and harassers discount or invalidate the claim of harassment by the victim. While it may seem as if this process shouldn't happen, it does, and reports by victims show the pattern.

Denial is one of the most common forms of discounting by the victims. They say to themselves and/or others: "He didn't really mean it that way," "I must be misinterpreting his intentions," "Surely he's not really coming on to me," "This can't be happening; I must be crazy." Most people would think that when the harassment continues the victim would finally stop denying that it's happening. Sexual harassment is embarrassing and difficult for the victim to deal with, especially when the harasser is the supervisor or a co-worker who is liked. Denial allows the victim to avoid dealing with a very painful situation.

Other victims recognize that it's happening but decide to do nothing. They say, "It's just part of working here. You've got to expect some of it." These employees become irritable, touchy, and less effective in their work. They usually find that the problem does not go away but in fact gets worse.

Another common trap is that victims blame themselves for causing the harassment. They will often try to look less attractive in their dress and general appearance, feeling, "If I look less sexy, he'll leave me alone." In serious harassment cases the victim finds that how he or she looks has very little to do with it and the harassment continues. Harassment is not the victim's fault.

Victims sometimes blame others who are not even involved in the harassment situation. Blaming other women or men in the office for "causing" the harasser to harass is the pattern. This may be because it is so difficult or risky for the employee to confront the harasser directly.

Last, employees who are sexually harassed may try a coping mechanism of avoidance: they avoid certain people, jobs, or areas. When this happens, the employee is spending time trying to cope with inappropriate or illegal behavior. Obviously, his or her job performance is affected. To some victims this seems like, or is, the only realistic alternative.

None of these mechanisms is a solution. To stop sexual harassment, it must be brought out in the open with both the victim and the harasser. Victims must recognize sexual harassment for what it is, understand that it is not their fault, and know that they have a right to complain and get it stopped.

Responses of Harassers

Harassers will also try, consciously or unconsciously, to invalidate or discount victims' claims of sexual harassment by one or more of the following:

When confronted either by the victim or by someone else trying to help stop the harassment, the harasser will often say that the victim has no sense of humor and can't take a joke. A joke is usually funny to the people involved, and harassment victims are saying that the jokes or remarks are not funny. They are offensive, embarrassing, and many times degrading.

Harassers will also say that the employee who feels victimized is not a good sport and just "can't take it." Sometimes hazing and teasing are a part of the social initiation that goes on in the workplace. However, when this testing or teasing is about sex and it becomes degrading or offensive, it must be stopped.

Some harassers will try to deny or reinterpret their intentions or motives, claiming that the victim misinterpreted their actions. This is often tied in with what is called the "I was just" game. When the offending employee is asked or told to stop a certain behavior, he or she will claim that "I was just being nice," "I was just teasing," "I was just complimenting her," and so forth. If the instance does involve a misinterpretation of behavior, the receiving employee is made aware of the misunderstanding, and the sending employee knows to be careful of that kind of behavior in the future.

Perhaps the most common form of discounting by the harasser is blaming the victim for causing the harassment. The logic of this argument says that the victim actually makes the harasser do things. Comments are often made that the victim "asked for it," "started it," "wants it," or that the victim is a "bitch," "troublemaker," or some other derogatory category.

In talking about harassers, it should be made clear, again, that most people are not sexual harassers. Most men and women treat each other in very appropriate ways. It's a small minority of people causing the serious problems. But we can talk about three kinds of harassers or potential harassers: unaware, insensitive, and hard-core.

Probably all of us at one time or another fall into the *unaware* category. People say and do things that embarrass others or make them feel bad. But when we see that others are embarrassed, we stop whatever it is we're doing, and then we too usually are embarrassed by the situation. It might be more accurate to call this kind of behavior inappropriate instead of harassment, because it is unintentional and can be stopped by the victim.

More serious are the *insensitive* harassers. They know that their behavior is offensive to others because they've been asked and told to stop. These people continue anyway, for whatever reasons of their own. It will take someone with more power, like a supervisor or manager, or the policy statement combined with discipline to get this behavior stopped.

Hard-core harassers are usually angry and hostile, and they continually degrade, intimidate, embarrass, and abuse their co-workers. These individuals are being taken out of the system—being terminated and replaced—because of their unwillingness to change their behavior. Organizations can't afford to keep these people and run the risk of substantial liability.

CHAPTER SUMMARY

A simple sexual harassment complaint—one that involves only the complaining employee and the alleged harasser—can be handled and resolved by a supervisor or manager working only with the two people.

A complex complaint—one that calls for an actual investigation—is usually handled by a human resources professional or an outside investigator, and involves the two employees as well other employees as witnesses or victims of harassment.

Handling a simple complaint consists of four elements: interviews with the complaining employee and the alleged harasser, an assessment of the incident, a review of the available records, and appropriate action.

When assessing the behavior that occurred, the supervisor or manager must take into account all the circumstances, or the "totality of the situation."

The supervisor or manager must make sure that the action taken against any employee is appropriate for the infraction: the punishment must fit the crime.

Disciplinary action can be mild, moderate, or severe, but should generally follow progressive disciplinary procedures.

The supervisor or manager handling a complaint should be familiar with the typical responses and patterns of behavior of victims and harassers.

5

Training and Education: The Most Important Steps of All

As soon as I started the workshop, I knew that I'd made a mistake—a big mistake. Actually, the big mistake consisted of a number of little mistakes that added up to one giant problem. There I was, standing in front of ninety power company linemen. From the look of things, all ninety were very much wanting to be somewhere—anywhere—else, and at least half of them were observably hostile.

The men were coming off shift, and they were cold and tired and dirty. They just wanted to go home, and they couldn't believe they were going to have to sit through a three-hour session on sexual harassment—especially since, as they said, "we don't even work with any of 'em"—" 'em" meaning women.

Needless to say, they weren't the only ones who couldn't imagine how the ninety-one of us were going to get through the next three hours, but there we were, and we had to get on with the show. We were in the all-purpose room at the line headquarters in a rural part of the state. The room was long and narrow and very cold. It was their locker room–changing room–lunchroom–game room. The floor was bare, cold concrete, the walls were lined with lockers, and the men were sitting on metal folding chairs about six chairs across and so far back I could hardly see the last row.

As I said, there we were. By now some of those mistakes I mentioned should be coming into focus. One, it was just me and them. No supervisor, no manager, no human resources person from corporate. In fact, the supervisor who had introduced me at the start of the session by saying "Uh, well, we're gonna talk about sexual harassment today, and here she is . . ." (I swear to you, that's exactly what he said) had just left.

Two, we were all extremely uncomfortable, both physically and mentally. It seemed freezing in the room, their chairs were hard and cold, and we were obviously off to a bad start. Now for the ugly . . .

During the first half hour of the session, I was trying to make what I thought was a simple and noncontroversial point. I said that it's often difficult for the victim of harassment to speak up, for fear of ridicule, retaliation, hostility, whatever. I went on to say that it's up to all of us to help create an environment at work in which people can speak up so we can get it stopped.

An older man sitting in the front row, about a foot from where I was standing, kept pounding his fist on the side of his chair and saying, "By God, it's not sexual harassment unless she says so!" over and over. Regardless of my response, he repeated the chair-pounding and by-Godding.

After a few minutes, a young man at the back of the room stepped out from the group he'd been standing with. There were plenty of empty chairs, but I've found that those who really don't want to be at the workshop refuse to sit—so they can make a quick getaway, I suppose—or they sit or stand as far away from me and the front of the room as possible. So when he shouted, "Hey! Hey, lady!", I have to admit, my heart skipped a beat, anticipating a not-too-friendly encounter.

Then the good part. This young man said, in a thick southern drawl, "Everybody in here is sayin', 'If she don't like it she oughta say somethin' ' or 'If he don't like it he oughta say somethin'.' Well, I think the men in here oughta look around for a minute. If I was a woman in this room right now, I wouldn't say shit."

You could have heard a pin drop, and I made what seemed like my first good move of the day. I said nothing. What was there to say? He had made the point beautifully. I thought of offering to pay him to join me in all my workshops and pop up at the appropriate time to make the point again. Our bad start took a turn for the better. I learned some important lessons from the workshop that day:

- Always educate your supervisors or managers ahead of time so they provide a positive, supportive introduction to you, the trainer, and, more important, to the subject of sexual harassment and the overall training effort.
- Make your trainees as comfortable as possible, physically and mentally. Don't use inadequate facilities, no matter what. Provide refreshments, chairs, and tables to sit around. Act as the host to those attending your sessions.
- Be careful of assumptions you make about your trainees. The fellow I had assumed was hostile, standing at the back of the room, turned out to be one of the most helpful, supportive people in the session.

But the biggest lesson I learned is that there are three parts to any training program: content—the actual material or information that's covered in the workshop; process—the way in which that information is delivered (lecture, videotape, case studies, etc.); and, often overlooked, the learning environment—the atmosphere for learning that the trainer can help create. All three of these aspects of effective training are covered in this chapter.

PLANNING AND PREPARATION FOR TRAINING

It's worth repeating here that those organizations that have effectively dealt with the sexual harassment issue have comprehensive programs that include six key elements: top management support, a policy statement, procedures for handling complaints, employee training, effective complaint resolution, and follow-though. In a sense, the first three—management support, the policy, and procedures—can be viewed as the basic planning and preparation for implementation of the fourth element—training. The first three elements must in place before effective employee training can occur.

Management Support

Top management's attitude toward sexual harassment can be a major obstacle to the effectiveness of training and education. A good training program takes time, effort, and energy on the part of the trainer and other individuals responsible for the sessions. It also requires the commitment of considerable time and resources on the part of the entire organization, not only in setting up the training, but in employee time to attend the sessions.

Sometimes providing additional information and education to the managers themselves during a management briefing can help sensitize them to the problem and convince them of the need for general employee training. Other companies have used informal survey results from their own employees, showing the extent of the problem within their company or organization, to indicate the need for attention to the problem.

Just remember, whatever it takes to get management support—additional information, management training, or even the occasional threat from the top—this support for the sexual harassment training program is the first and most critical step in making it effective. Without it, training just won't work.

Policy Statement

A written, posted policy statement should precede the training effort. The policy should explicitly address sexual harassment and should be more specific than a general antiharassment or nondiscrimination statement (see Chapter 3).

The policy demonstrates management's understanding and support of the issue as well as its commitment to eliminating the problem. It also establishes the procedures for handling instances of harassment. Since the procedures are part of the training session content, the policy must be completed prior to training.

Grievance Procedures

The grievance or complaint procedures, both formal and informal, should also be covered in all training sessions. These procedures increase the organization's chances of dealing with the problem internally, before complaints are made to an external agency. The procedures don't need to be complicated but should be established prior to training (see Chapter 3).

IMPLEMENTING EMPLOYEE TRAINING

The training program should include a number of presentations and workshops for all employees. *The program should be divided into separate sessions for executive-level management, supervisors and other managers, and general-level employees,* because they all have different responsibilities.

The program should not include separate sessions for men and women. This would help perpetuate the misconception that most men are guilty of harassment, that only women are victims, and that this is a divisive issue—a battle of the sexes. Both men and women must hear the same information regarding the sexual harassment issue. Both have the same rights and responsibilities.

The training should begin with top management and end with general employees. If this isn't possible, the sessions can run concurrently. The entire program should be completed in a timely fashion.

It is critical that all levels of employees be included at some time in the training and educational effort. Some organizations have chosen to have professional trainers, either from within the organization or outside consultants, train the management group and the supervisors, and then have the supervisors educate the general-level employees. This works well where the supervisors are willing and able to provide information on sexual harassment and to answer sometimes difficult and sensitive questions. Where the supervisors lack the skill or are unwilling to address this issue with their employees, certain groups of employees never get the necessary information.

Once it has been decided who will receive training, schedules can be set up for supervisors and general employees. Schedules can indicate date, time, and maximum number of participants, in the form of a sign-up sheet. With large numbers of employees, this allows people to attend the most convenient session.

Supervisors can also help in scheduling their own employees and should be allowed flexibility to accommodate work schedules. It's not necessary for employees who work together to attend the sessions as a group. There may, in fact, be some benefit in their hearing other employees' points of view.

The notice or memo that goes before and/or with the schedules should indicate management's strong and positive support of the effort against sexual harassment. It should briefly explain the purpose and content of the sessions, and indicate that attendance is mandatory. No employee should be excused from attending a session. The announcement is the first step in the training process and begins to set the tone for the entire program. Make sure that it is written so it is straightforward but not threatening.

Approach Used in Training

The primary emphasis of sexual harassment training should be on behavioral changes on the job, and secondarily on attitudinal changes. Attitudinal changes are beneficial but optional; behavioral changes are mandatory. The trainer should conduct the sessions to bring about behavior changes through increased awareness and understanding and, where necessary, skill development.

Each workshop should include teaching methods (lecture, presentation, discussion, question-and-answer, exercises) most appropriate to the employees being trained. Each session should be tailored to the employees' needs.

Author Charles Watson says that to obtain voluntary behavioral change in individuals, it is necessary to help them through four levels of learning: knowing about, understanding, acceptance, and the ability to apply and make changes (skill development). Each step requires more time and energy on the part of the trainer and participants, and each step requires different training techniques.

The *knowing about* level requires brief explanations and introduction by the trainer of concepts of sexual harassment and discrimination. *Understanding*—meaning more in-depth knowledge of the reasons and rationales of the harassment issues— requires more lengthy presentations and the opportunity to ask questions and get answers. These first two levels of learning relate primarily to providing employees with additional knowledge: information and input.

The third level, *acceptance*, is the attitudinal level. Before being able to voluntarily apply their knowledge to change their negative behavior, people must, to some degree, accept the truth or validity of the information already provided. This requires lecture and question-and-answer, combined with group discussions, debates (controlled by the trainer), confronting, role-playing, and exercises.

In human relations areas, especially controversial areas such as sexual harassment, employees often have as much or more effect in changing each other's attitudes (acceptance of knowledge) as do the trainers. So, at the acceptance level, small and large group discussions generated from exercises can be used very effectively.

The fourth level is actual *skill development*—the ability to apply what they've learned and to change their behavior—and it requires the use of all training techniques, including lecture, question-and-answer, discussion, demonstration, practice, and feedback. At this level, employees will learn the how-to's of handling harassment and discrimination on an interpersonal level.

Usually, in an all-employee sexual harassment training program, more emphasis will be given to the management/supervisory-level employees because of their responsibility to recognize and handle harassment and because of the organization's legal liability where supervisors are concerned. The manager/supervisor workshops should be designed to take them through all four levels of learning, from knowing about to ability to apply.

The top-level management briefing is to provide basic knowledge and understanding of the issue and should be used only for truly top-level management. All other managers should attend the management/supervisory sessions. Since people at the executive level are somewhat accustomed to laws, rules, and regulations, additional time convincing them of the importance of the issue may not be necessary. If it should prove necessary, they should attend a management/supervisor workshop.

The general-employee presentation is to provide basic knowledge and understanding, since they need to know what sexual harassment is and what to do about it. They have the option of going to a supervisor for additional help.

Throughout the entire program, the topic of sexual harassment must be approached as a work-related productivity issue and not solely a social, moral, or feminist problem. Costs to the work environment and legal liability must continually be emphasized.

Primary Subject Areas

There are five basic subject areas or questions that must be addressed in a sexual harassment training program. These five areas should be included in the programs for all levels: executive, management/supervisory, and general employee. More or less emphasis can be given to each subject depending on the level of the employees.

1. Introduction
2. Why are we here?
3. What is harassment?
4. Why should I worry about it?
5. What am I supposed to do?

INTRODUCTION

The introduction is primarily for use in the supervisory- and general-employee-level sessions. It should be written by the trainer himself or herself so it begins to individualize the session to the style of the trainer.

The purpose of the introduction is to set the tone of the

session, to indicate the parameters of the workshop and the trainer's expectations of the participants, and, as much as possible, to put the participants at ease and reduce defensiveness. To achieve its purposes, the introduction should include:

- An introduction of the issue of sexual harassment by a high-level person in the organization, to spell out the organization's stand, the importance of these sessions, and the organization's expectation that all employees will participate fully and with respect for each other and their differing perceptions.
- An introduction of the trainer, if necessary, by this same high-level person.
- An introduction of the trainer, if necessary, by himself or herself, indicating the trainer's background, experience, and approach to training.
- A statement that the purpose of this session is to learn about and try to understand a complex issue and not to embarrass or punish anyone.
- A statement that the trainer has information to present and will stop for questions at the end of each section.
- A "details" statement about time frame, when breaks will occur, and where restrooms are. Then ask if there are questions before the session starts.

WHY ARE WE HERE?
Often employees don't understand or believe that harassment and discrimination exist or that they are real problems. A history of the issue and an overview of the problem begin the process of addressing employees' lack of awareness, giving them the background and foundation for understanding the issues presented in the rest of the program.

A brief statement regarding the sexual harassment problem in this particular organization can also be presented here. Details of individual cases should be omitted, but this serves to let employees know what their organization is like. If no instances have been reported, then the preventive nature of the training can be emphasized.

WHAT IS HARASSMENT?

Defining harassment is usually easier than actually recognizing it when it occurs, because it varies from situation to situation and from person to person. Employees must be able to distinguish between instances of behavior that are appropriate, inappropriate, and illegal. Considerable time should be given to understanding and developing the ability to make this distinction, particularly for supervisors, who often have to diagnose problem situations.

WHY SHOULD I WORRY ABOUT IT?

First, employees must be concerned about sexual harassment because of state and federal laws, as well as city and county policies and ordinances.

Second, and perhaps more important, are the negative costs and consequences that accrue to the organization and its employees—victims, co-workers, and harassers.

WHAT AM I SUPPOSED TO DO?

The training must take into account the unique responsibilities of employees at each level—management, supervisors, and general employees—and spell out specifically what is expected of them. The organization's own procedures should be included at this point.

For additional help in setting up an employee training program on sexual harassment, see my book *Sexual Harassment: Training Manual.*

CHAPTER SUMMARY

The three parts of an effective training program are content—the material or information that's covered in the training; process— the way in which the information is delivered; and learning envi- ronment—the atmosphere for learning that the trainer creates.

Management support, a policy statement, and procedures for getting and handling complaints should be in place before a training program is undertaken.

Sexual harassment training should be divided into separate sessions for top-level management, managers and supervisors, and general employees.

The program should not include separate sessions for men and women.

The emphasis in training should be on changing behavior first and attitudes second.

Five subjects should be addressed in all sexual harassment training sessions: Introducing the subject. Why are we here? What is harassment? Why should I worry about it? What am I supposed to do?

6

The Most-Asked Questions

Anybody who has worked in the area of sexual harassment for any time at all will tell you that the same questions are asked time and time again. Unfortunately, it's sometimes just one or two people who ask the same questions over and over—usually because they didn't get the answer they wanted the first time.

But more often the same questions are asked repeatedly by different people, simply because there is so little real knowledge about sexual harassment out there. One reporter was heard to say that, in her opinion, all that the polls about sexual harassment reveal is the ignorance of the pollees.

Anyhow, when you hear these questions, it's always nice to have some straightforward, fairly concise answers, so here they are—the questions and some answers.

What's This All About Anyway?

Title VII of the 1964 Civil Rights Act as amended says that men and women must be treated equally in all job matters. In other words, discrimination in employment (such as hiring, firing, pay, promotion, benefits) based on sex is illegal. This law is enforced by the Equal Employment Opportunity Commission (EEOC), which is a federal agency.

On November 10, 1980, the EEOC's Guidelines on sexual harassment became effective. These amended Guidelines reaffirmed EEOC's position that sexual harassment is a form of sex discrimination and therefore is an "unlawful employment practice" under Title VII of the Civil Rights Act. In short, sexual harassment is illegal.

The Guidelines are broad and sometimes difficult to interpret. But since they define what is legal and illegal for organizations and their employees, everyone—supervisors and managers, executives, and other employees—must have a clear and complete understanding of them.

So What Do the Guidelines Say?

Those sections of the EEOC Guidelines that are important to supervisors, managers, and other employees are summarized below:

Section A: Sexual harassment consists of unwelcome sexual advances, requests for sexual favors, and other verbal or physical conduct of a sexual nature. Such behavior is illegal:

- When it is part of a manager's or supervisor's decision to hire or fire someone.
- When it is used to make other employment decisions such as those about pay, promotion, or job assignment.
- When it interferes with an employee's work performance.
- When it creates an intimidating, hostile, or offensive work environment.

Section B: In deciding sexual harassment cases, the EEOC will look at all the circumstances on a case-by-case basis.

Section C: An employer is responsible for harassment by its supervisory personnel whether or not it knows about the actions, and whether or not it approves or disapproves of such behavior.

Section D: An employer is responsible for harassment by co-workers if it knows or should know about the actions and does not take immediate and appropriate action to correct the situation.

Section E: An employer may be responsible for harassment of its employees by people who are not its employees when the harassment occurs in the line of work and the employer knows or should know about it and fails to take immediate and appropriate action.

Section F: Employers should take all necessary steps to prevent sexual harassment from occurring in the first place.

Section G: If an employee submits to sexual requests and gains benefits from that, the employer may be sued for sex discrimination by other employees who were equally qualified and denied those benefits.

Exactly What Is Sexual Harassment?

Sexual harassment is deliberate or repeated behavior of a sexual nature, or of a sex-based nature, that is unwelcome, not asked for, and not returned. The behavior can be verbal, nonverbal, or physical. It is deliberate—not happening by accident but by someone's intent—and/or it is repeated—happening more than once.

Examples of verbal harassment could include sexual comments, suggestions, jokes, or innuendos. Nonverbal harassment could include suggestive looks, leering, or ogling. Physical harassment could include "accidentally" brushing against someone's body, "friendly" pats, squeezes, or pinches, and forced sexual relations.

While some harassing behavior is easy to identify, such as an explicit proposition backed by the threat of job loss, other behavior such as flirting or joking is sometimes more difficult to define. The key idea in the definition to help people decide whether behavior is or is not sexual harassment is the word *unwelcome.* If co-workers enjoy the mutual exchange of suggestive comments, their behavior may be permissible; however, if any employee finds the behavior or comments offensive or is made the object of unwelcome sexual attention, the behavior can be considered sexual harassment.

The word *unwelcome* places responsibility on the receiver to tell the sender or a supervisor or manager that the behavior is unwanted. It also places responsibility on supervisors to watch and listen carefully for clues to unwanted attention. Whether the harassment is from a supervisor to subordinate or from one co-worker to another, it is illegal behavior under federal, state, and most local laws and ordinances.

Why Should I Worry About It?

First of all, it is part of a supervisor's and manager's job to see that their employer stays within the law, that neither they nor their subordinates engage in illegal behavior. Because employers have a legal responsibility to stop and prevent sexual harassment, their supervisors and managers also share that responsibility.

The unwelcome sexual advances of a supervisor or manager are more likely to be immediately illegal, since the harassment may be linked to the subordinate's job status. It is illegal for a subordinate's job, pay, promotion, firing, layoff, or any other term or condition of employment to depend on a positive response to a supervisor's sexual advances or requests. It is a form of unlawful sex discrimination.

In addition, employers may be held responsible for the behavior of their supervisors even when they have forbidden such behavior and even when they do not know it is taking place. In other words, under the concept of "strict liability," when supervisors sexually harass employees by use of their supervisory power, the employer may be held liable and sued, even if the employer told the supervisor beforehand not to harass and even if the employer was unaware that it was happening.

In some cases, employees harassed by supervisors may file suit immediately, without allowing their employer the opportunity to remedy the situation. Employers risk considerable liability for supervisory harassment.

Finally, when employers discover that sexual harassment by nonsupervisory employees is occurring or has occurred, they are required to take appropriate remedial action immediately to correct that situation. This action could include reprimands, negative performance reviews, disciplinary actions, or even termination of the offending employee. Every employee—managers, supervisors, and all others—must be concerned about sexual harassment on the job.

What Should Supervisors and Managers Do?

Supervisors and managers have two primary responsibilities. First, they are required to stop sexual harassment among their subordinates by recognizing and dealing with cases as they occur. Specifically, this means handling each complaint of harassment in a fair and equitable fashion and disciplining the employee who engaged in harassing behavior. Supervisors and managers are also responsible for preventing future occurrences of harassment by informing and educating subordinates and correcting the offensive behavior.

Most organizations provide supervisors with established disciplinary procedures to handle employees who break rules and to correct their behavior. Generally, the procedures follow a standard form such as (1) talking with the employee who broke the rule (first verbal warning), (2) second verbal warning, (3) written warning, (4) probation, and (5) termination. Each time the employee breaks the rule, the disciplinary action is more severe.

Since sexual harassment is on-the-job behavior that is inappropriate, against employer policy, and illegal, supervisors should treat it as they would any other instance of serious employee misconduct, following their organization's disciplinary procedures. Special methods of disciplining the harasser do not need to be established.

When disciplinary action is taken against a sexual harasser, that action must be appropriate and fit the severity of the infraction. For example, a verbal warning to discipline an employee for attempted rape or physical abuse of a co-worker would certainly not be considered appropriate. Gross misconduct requires more severe discipline.

Is It Really That Big a Problem?

Yes. The costs of sexual harassment are high for both the employer and the employee who is harassed. Losing a sexual harassment suit is as costly and damaging to an organization as losing any other EEOC action. Recent court actions against employers have awarded money to harassed employees for back pay, reinstatement, attorneys' fees, and unemployment compensation in amounts ranging from five thousand dollars to several million dollars.

Other important but less obvious costs to the organization result from the effects of harassment on the victim. Studies show that sexually harassed employees may feel embarrassed, demeaned, or intimidated, and that they suffer physically and emotionally. Their symptoms, such as headaches, stomach problems, and inability to concentrate, may show up as increased absenteeism, inefficiency, and loss of productivity. Since many harassed employees quit their jobs, the costs of turnover—recruiting, rehiring, and retraining—are also substantial.

It is also possible for sexual harassment to lower the productivity of an entire work group. Co-workers who see another employee being harassed may not speak up, but may still be affected in terms of their own lowered morale, decreased motivation, and job performance.

Aren't Those Just a Few Isolated Cases?

No. Studies and surveys indicate that as many as 88 percent of all working women and as many as 15 percent of working men have experienced some form of sexual harassment. The problem is not limited to any particular group but occurs in all jobs, at all salary levels, in all age and racial groups, and in both the public and private sectors.

Don't Women Harass Men, Too?

Yes. However, the majority of harassers are men. More than 95 percent of all sexual harassment cases involve men as the offenders, and less than 5 percent involve women harassers.

Those 5 percent of the cases in which men are the victims of harassment by women are the exceptions rather than the general trend. The greatest number of victims are women.

Does This Mean It's Illegal to Ask for a Date?

No. Employees are within their legal rights to ask other employees for dates and to be friendly with them. The EEOC and the laws are not concerned with what happens between consenting adults. The concern is with unwelcome sexual behavior that has a negative impact on an employee's job or career.

The situation for supervisors and subordinates is somewhat

different than for co-workers. It is when the supervisor's requests for dates or sexual favors are unwelcome and are made a condition of employment (pay, promotion, etc.) that they become illegal. The key words are *unwelcome* and *linked to employment*.

Even though supervisors may ask for dates or date subordinates, it is an unwise practice. A case in which a supervisor asks a subordinate for a date, the subordinate turns down the request, and later the supervisor gives a poor performance review or even fires that subordinate certainly opens the door for the question of sexual harassment to be raised. The same kind of situation could occur when the two were dating and the relationship ended. It is not advisable for supervisors to date their subordinates.

As for co-workers, it is when their requests for dates or sexual favors are unwelcome or create an offensive work environment that they become illegal. Asking for a date once or twice is obviously not against the law. But repeatedly asking or pressuring for dates after the other person has said no can be defined as behavior that is unwelcome and offensive and interferes with getting work done. That kind of behavior is sexual harassment. The key words for co-workers are *unwelcome, offensive environment,* and *interferes.*

In both situations, for supervisors and co-workers, the word *unwelcome* plays an important part. When employees indicate that the sexual behavior directed toward them is unwanted, then it must be stopped immediately.

Can't I Open a Door or Light a Cigarette?

Opening a door or lighting someone's cigarette is social behavior that is part of society's rules of etiquette, more for use in social situations than on the job. These rules, which are rapidly changing, define how "gentlemanly" men and "ladylike" women should act and be treated. They are what people define as "good

manners" and are not usually sexual behavior. Under most circumstances good manners would not be regarded as sexual
harassment.

However, an employee may carry such "manners" to extremes
with a co-worker of the opposite sex and annoy, embarrass, or
degrade that other employee. Then it is inappropriate on-the-job
behavior, although it may not be illegal. This kind of inappropriate behavior may signal supervisors and managers that illegal
sexual harassment is also taking place.

The idea of "unwelcome behavior" again helps clarify what is
and what is not appropriate at work. When employees do not
want or welcome the behavior that another is directing toward
them, even if it is supposedly "mannerly" behavior, that behavior should be stopped. This simple rule can help all employees
prevent many potential problems and conflict situations from
escalating.

What's Wrong with Complimenting Somebody?

Nothing is wrong with complimenting other employees, especially when those compliments help with their job performance,
relate to their work, or make them feel good. But comments and
compliments that embarrass, degrade, or intimidate are inappropriate on the job and should not be allowed. Compliments that
are sexual, repeated, and unwanted are illegal and must not be
allowed.

Employees should be aware that the person giving a compliments can twist its meaning and send a sexual message through
body language, tone of voice, sarcasm, or facial expression. Then,
when challenged, the harassing employee will deny that the intent
was to send a sexual message. Employees should be careful of
such situations.

With sexual harassment, the harassed employee defines the

offense. When employees indicate that the behavior directed toward them is sexual and unwanted, it must be stopped immediately.

Isn't It Just That Some People Can't Take a Joke?

A genuine joke is usually funny to all the people involved. Sexual harassment is not a joke and is not funny to the people who are its victims. It is unwanted behavior that is repeated over and over again. It annoys, irritates, angers, and degrades, and it goes beyond teasing and good-natured fun. Few people would define continued and repeated embarrassment and intimidation of another as a joke.

Whose Fault Is It?

There are many reasons why sexual harassment is a problem, and many ideas about where to lay the blame. One of the most widespread myths is that it is the fault of the people who are harassed, that the victims themselves cause it to happen. Comments are often made that "they asked for it," "they started it," or "they wear their clothes [pants/shirt/blouse/skirt] too tight [loose/low/high, etc.]."

The truth is that the fault lies with the harasser. Some employees are simply unaware that their behavior is offensive, and when asked to stop, either by the offended employee or by a supervisor, they stop. Some employees are less sensitive to the feelings and wants of others and continue with their offending behavior until more or less forced to stop, usually by the direct orders of a supervisor or by a threat from management. Still others, the hard-core harassers, deliberately and repeatedly act in ways that embarrass, intimidate, or degrade other employees. All are guilty, but it is the less sensitive and the hard-core harassers who cause serious problems for their organizations, their supervisors, and their co-workers.

A second myth is that most men are sexual harassers. The truth is that men who sexually harass women are in the minority. Most men behave appropriately toward their female co-workers and subordinates. It is a relatively small number of men who are causing a great number of problems.

Don't They Really Like All That Attention?

Some people may in fact like sexual attentions at work. When an employee genuinely enjoys, welcomes, and returns the sexual attention of a co-worker, it is not sexual harassment but rather a mutual exchange.

On the other hand, some employees do not like or want to engage in sexual behavior such as joking or flirting on the job. They want to do their work free from this kind of activity. Supervisors and managers must ensure that the rights of and wants of these employees are observed. Their right to say "no" to such behavior from others is a legal right protected by law.

Abusive, degrading, and intimidating sexual behavior is a different matter. No one likes or enjoys receiving this kind of attention. It is both inappropriate and illegal.

How Can I Be Sure It's Sexual Harassment?

To recognize sexual harassment, first decide if the behavior in question is job-related. Does it go toward getting the work done? If the answer is "yes," the behavior is appropriate and will probably not cause problems. If the answer is "no" and the behavior is social, then consider the following:

- Is the behavior directed toward employees of one gender only—only men or only women?
- Is it courting, flirting, or sexual behavior?
- Has the employee receiving the attention objected in any way, said or indicated "no," "stop," "I don't like it"? Has

the employee been asked if the attention is objected to or unwanted?

- Is the behavior or similar behavior repeated? Has it happened before?
- Does the offending employee behave this way deliberately, on purpose?
- Does the behavior interfere with the receiving employee's work performance?
- Does it create an environment that is hostile, intimidating, or offensive for an employee?
- Does the employee feel demeaned, degraded, or embarrassed by the behavior?

If the answer to several of the questions is "yes," the behavior may well be considered sexual harassment. The EEOC Guidelines also spell out conditions of harassment.

So What Can I Do?

All employees can play a part in stopping inappropriate and offensive behavior on the job. Watching and listening for indications from co-workers that attention is unwelcome is the first step in preventing problems. Victims of sexual harassment are being told and encouraged to say "no" to unwelcome behavior. Their co-workers must be aware of and observe those objections.

Second, employees must let their co-workers know that they take the problem of sexual harassment seriously and that they do not approve. Employees must do more than not harass: they must actively speak up and support their co-workers who are victims.

7

Steps Forward for All Employees

Each and every one of us has a responsibility to stop and prevent sexual harassment—at work and in other parts of our lives as well. Every time we don't speak up to the person bothering us, every time we don't say something to the person who we know is bothering others, every time we laugh or snicker or discount the issue, we become part of the problem.

The steps forward that we as individuals can take are sometimes difficult and may even be costly to us personally, but there are also steps that are simple and not too tough.

STEPS FOR MANAGERS

Notify all employees with a written, posted policy statement that sexual harassment is illegal and will not be tolerated. See the sample policy statement in Chapter 3.

Talk with subordinates about the problem of sexual harassment clearly, directly, and seriously. Answer questions and spell out what is expected of employees.

Tell subordinates that sexual harassment will be treated as serious, illegal employee misconduct and that harassers will be dealt with firmly.

Tell subordinates that employees who think they are being sexually harassed by their supervisor should talk with a higher-level supervisor, manager, equal employment opportunity counselor, affirmative action officer, or other designated person.

Establish lines of communication with subordinates and make it known that an open-door policy exists for sexual harassment problems.

Be alert to what is happening between employees; try to anticipate problems.

Include sexual harassment awareness as part of the orientation and training of new employees.

Deal with sexual harassment problems promptly. This will go far in preventing future occurrences.

Designate a person within the organization who is sensitive to and understands the issue of sexual harassment to work with employees who are harassed or who think they may be victims.

Establish and make known to all employees the grievance procedure for complaints of sexual harassment.

STEPS FOR SUPERVISORS

There are four circumstances in which supervisors will have to deal with sexual harassment: when a complaint is made to them, when they see or hear about behavior that they think might be harassment, when they see or hear about behavior that they know is harassment, or when they engage in behavior with others that they think might be offensive. The do's and don't for supervisors are listed here.

If an Employee Complains to a Supervisor About Sexual Harassment

DO

Listen to the employee and find out what action the employee wants to take. The employee may only want to tell the supervisor about it, to get more information about his or her rights, or to handle it alone.

Offer to help by talking to the offending employee privately or by meeting with the two of them together, if the victim wants the supervisor's help in resolving the problem.

Document briefly for yourself the who, what, when, and where of your discussion with the complaining employee. Notify your supervisor and/or the personnel/equal employment opportunity office. Follow up by checking back with the employee. Repeat this step as necessary.

Encourage the harassed employee to say "no" to the offender (most inappropriate behavior can be stopped this way), but you may not require the employee to handle the situation.

Treat the offender's behavior as you would any other instance of serious misconduct by following the organization's disciplinary procedures.

Correct and stop the inappropriate behavior immediately. Most harassed employees file suits as a last resort because they were unable to get the sexual harassment stopped.

DON'T

Tell the harassed employee to ignore it; 75 percent of the cases get worse when ignored.

Assume the victim asked for it or is at fault.

Make light of, laugh at, or discount the victim.

Tell the victim to embarrass the harasser, to get physical in return, to outwit the other.

Let the behavior continue. It is illegal.

If the Supervisor Sees Possibly Sexually Harassing Behavior but Is Not Sure

DO

Ask the employee receiving such behavior if it is harassing or offensive. Employees may need to be told that they do not have to put up with such behavior from others.

DON'T

Let it wait until "next time"; it will probably get worse.

If the Supervisor Sees Definitely Sexually Harassing Behavior

DO

Talk with the offender and correct the behavior immediately.

DON'T

Wait for the victim to complain before taking action.

If You Think Something You Do (or Have Done in the Past) as an Employee or Co-worker Bothered or Offended Another Person

DO

Stop the behavior—do not do it again—or ask the other person, quietly and privately, if the behavior was or is bothersome. If he or she says "no," ask again, to be certain.

DON'T

Assume that the person does not mind or likes the behavior since he or she has not objected.

STEPS FOR EMPLOYEES

So it happened again today. It really seemed minor the first couple of times. All along you've known it was a problem, but today you started thinking about it seriously: sexual harassment. Could it really be happening to you? Who'd ever believe . . .

So now, what to do? You know the standard options: tell the jerk to cut it out or else, talk to your boss (or the boss's boss), file a complaint, or, better yet, the big one—a lawsuit. Go to court!

Of course, it's not that simple. For most women and men who experience sexual harassment the goals are the same: to get it stopped, to keep their job, and, equally important, to maintain their effectiveness in their job and organization. Some of the standard options may achieve one goal at the cost of another.

What's needed in a situation like this, whether you're at the top, middle, or bottom of the corporate ladder, is balance and strategy. If ever a game plan was needed, now's the time.

Before taking action, use these ideas to help yourself gain perspective and formulate a plan for resolving this situation within your company or organization—for the benefit of everyone involved.

1. Admit that a problem exists; don't deny it to yourself. You may choose, as a tactic, to ignore it and see if it goes away, but choosing to ignore it is quite different from denying that it exists. Denial will only compound an already confused situation.

2. Recognize sexual harassment for what it is—deliberate or repeated sexual behavior that's unwelcome. Ask yourself if the behavior is sexual or directed at you because of your gender. Is it happening on purpose or is it accidental? Is it repeated over and over? Is it knowingly unwelcome? Have you said or indicated that you don't like it? Do you participate in or initiate the behavior?

3. Keep in mind the most important point, that whether the behavior is a truly major issue (usually the more obvious kinds, like "put out or get out") or less severe but still inappropriate (occasional yet repeated jokes or innuendoes), it's a problem that usually won't just go away.

4. Remember that whatever kind of behavior it is, it's still costing everybody. You're paying the price with a higher stress level, and your job efficiency and effectiveness are mostly likely affected too. It's damaging to you, both personally and professionally. It needs to be stopped.

5. Keep in mind that your company or organization has an interest in stopping this kind of behavior at work. Sexual harassment can be damaging to an organization in terms of absenteeism, loss of productivity, and lowered morale and motivation.

6. Accept responsibility for taking part in solving the problem—not blame, but responsibility. Do something to take control of the bad situation that you're caught up in.

7. Calmly and in private, speak up and tell the person that you don't like his or her behavior. This is usually best, especially if it's the first time you've said something about it and if it's a less serious behavior.

8. Use an "I-statement," saying, for example: "*When you* call me 'honey' [touch me/tell me jokes, etc.]"—describing the behavior you don't like—"*I feel* very upset [embarrassed/angry/offended]"—saying what your feelings are—"*because* I want to be taken seriously [want to be treated as an equal/want respect, etc.]"—saying why it bothers you.

Sometimes it helps to write out your I-statement and rehearse it ahead of time.

9. Use the "broken-record technique" by acknowledging the person's response and then repeating your I statement. If the offending employee responds by saying that he or she didn't

mean to hurt your feelings, or you're too sensitive, etc., you can say "I understand that you didn't mean to hurt my feelings; however, when you . . . I felt . . . because. . . ." You do not need to change your original I-statement.

10. Request what you do or don't want by saying "Please always call me by my name [don't touch me/don't tell me those jokes]." Be specific.

11. Try this mini-plan once or twice. If you don't get results from the offending employee, you'll have to move to another step.

12. Ask a co-worker for support and even help in talking with the offender. Sometimes the offender can hear a message more clearly from a friend or buddy.

13. Go to a supervisor or manager to get additional help if the behavior does not stop.

14. Don't assume the behavior will stop if you ignore it. Seventy-five percent of the time, sexual harassment problems get worse when ignored.

15. Don't try to deal with severe harassment alone, even the first time. In serious cases, let someone in the company know about it immediately. Get help.

16. If a mini-plan doesn't work, or if the problem is more complex or serious, a more thorough plan might be called for. In that case, it's important to find and maintain your balance and perspective by looking at all the elements of the problem.

17. Examine the situation itself first. What does the other person say or do? What do you say or do? When, where, how often does it happen? Does it happen to others? On a scale of 1 to 10, how severe do you consider each event?

18. Write down the answers to these questions. Writing it down can help you clarify the issues and give yourself some objectivity. Write a description, as factual as possible, of each event.

19. Then take a look at the other person and write down your thoughts. What's going on with this person? Why is he or she treating you this way? Is it possible that the other person is unaware of the negative effects the behavior has on you? Is the other person trying to be friendly, joking, or perhaps truly attracted to you? Is this person aware of the effects of the behavior but uncaring—insensitive to your feelings or how you've asked to be treated? Or is this person treating you this way deliberately, maliciously, after your repeated objections?

20. Take a look at yourself. Have you been participating in the problem? Don't heap blame on yourself. That's a common trap. Just make sure you've looked at all sides and considered all aspects. How about your self-image at work? Does your image project how you want to be treated? Have you said "no" directly and specifically so there's no misunderstanding of your nonverbal messages?

21. Based on your analysis of the problem, now comes strategic planning. List all the ideas you can think of that would help stop the behavior and solve this problem. Then group or organize these ideas into three plans: Plan A, Plan B, and Plan C. Some of the ideas might be included in more than one of the plans.

22. Make your plans specific with regard to time, place, and actions. Think through all the consequences of each plan. Keep in mind that you have two simultaneous goals at this point: to get the behavior stopped and to maintain your effectiveness in your job.

23. Include other people in your plans. Don't try to be a hero and handle it all alone, especially with harassers who seem to be insensitive or malicious. Call on those friends, supervisors, or managers who you think can be of help.

24. Keep your plans flexible. The response of the harasser or of the manager or company representative may change your plans

and/or your timetable. Solving this problem involves other people and their time and effort, not just your own. Be reasonable.

25. Implement plan A, B, and/or C as necessary. If you've gone through the ideas above, you should be able to put your plan into action more calmly and confidently to get the results you want.

SO NOW WHAT?

Part of the problem is that many victims of sexual harassment don't speak up at all. For a variety of reasons, they just grin and bear it. Because they're unsure of what's going on, or they feel guilty or responsible, or they don't know how to handle it without risking losing, they do nothing. Sexual harassment usually won't go away when ignored; it usually gets worse.

The ideas given in this chapter obviously don't provide you with all the answers. Instead, they provide you with thoughts to help you come up with the answers for yourself—to think clearly and to devise plans to deal with the problem of sexual harassment this time, and, if necessary, next time.

It will take considerable thought and energy to come up with creative solutions for this sensitive problem. But only you can come up with the unique solutions that fit you and your organization and help you reach your personal and professional objectives. Remember to keep your supervisor, manager, or other appropriate company representative informed so he or she can work with you and help you resolve this problem.

Sexual harassment by its very growth as an issue is bringing about its own end. Organizations can't afford the financial costs of losing suits. Nor can they afford the production losses that sexual harassment causes, such as absenteeism, decreased efficiency, and higher turnover.

Victims should not try to just go away, either. They should

keep complaining, both men and women alike, to get this kind of behavior on the job stopped. It is a solvable problem. But we all have to work together on the issue as we do for any other problem at work, to get this problem solved.

8

What the Future Holds

Many people who work in the human rights field believe that in poor economic times all forms of harassment and discrimination occur more frequently. In fact, when people are worried and concerned about their economic well-being, negative behavior in general tends to rise, if for no other reason than the physical and emotional stresses associated with hard times.

These experts indicate that while the frequency of harassment rises, complaints of harassment and discrimination tend to decrease, since employees may fear that if they complain things will only get worse and they may lose the job they are lucky enough to have. Simultaneously, the number of individuals most likely to be harassed—minority employees—may be lower because of "last hired, first fired" patterns during layoffs.

Logically, the case for good economic times would seem to run counter to the poor-times scenario. While the actual incidence of harassing behavior may decrease, the number of reported cases may rise as victims feel more comfortable and secure about their jobs and thus more willing to complain. In addition, numbers of women and minorities in the workplace may be higher.

This kind of speculation provides food for thought as to the future and what it may hold for the issue of sexual harassment. General agreement is that complaints are likely to increase, at least for a number of years, as more women continue to enter the work force and the issue continues to gain widespread visibility.

More specifically, some expect to see an increase in the category of hostile environment complaints. Recent court decisions, including the 1986 Supreme Court decision in *Vinson* v. *Taylor*, have made this type of harassment claim more available to victims, and it may be the only recourse in many cases. As harassing behavior becomes more subtle, tangible job-related consequences, as in quid pro quo cases, will appear less often. It is then that the hostile, offensive work atmosphere affects the victim, interfering with the employee's ability to do the job. As hostile environment cases gain more visibility, the number of complaints against co-workers will undoubtedly increase as a result.

Also likely to increase are numbers of complaints in which a non-employee is the harasser. The courts have only recently begun to address this issue, and it will be of major concern as complaints are reported against customers, clients, and members of the general public.

One of the most obvious areas of change will be in the number of cases in which men are the victims of harassment. As it becomes more acceptable for men to object to certain kinds of sexual behavior from women, more will be more willing to speak up. And as the number of women in supervisory positions grows, the likelihood of female-to-male harassment increases.

A word of caution about numbers of male victims of female harassment: while some increase may be expected, women will continue to be the main victims of sexual harassment. Women are victimized not only because of the role structure of the work force and their economic vulnerability, but because of male and female roles in this society. The traditional male role of dominance and the female role of subordination in social relationships both complement and reinforce each other and spill over into the work environment.

It's unlikely that substantial numbers of women and men will exchange or reverse traditional roles so that women, in the dominant role, sexually harass great numbers of men in the subordinate role. The elements that contribute to male-to-female harassment—economic need, the role structure of the workplace, and stereotypical sex-role conditioning—can be expected to undergo major changes, but not necessarily reverses.

The Merit System Protection Board study indicated that most of the men complaining of sexual harassment were speaking of same-sex harassment from supervisors and co-workers. Since courts have noted that a finding of discrimination can be made if the supervisor is the same sex as the subordinate, homosexual-based claims of sexual harassment may become more frequent. The court in *Wright* v. *Methodist Youth Services* called homosexual harassment the "obverse side of the coin" of heterosexual harassment, so more litigation might also be expected.

Other areas of future concern are:

- The problem of the nonparticipant. Where some employees are willingly involved in sexual behavior but such behavior creates a hostile or offensive work environment for other workers who are not involved, do the offended employees have a right to object? A California court, ruling on a case in which the behavior in question was not directed at the complaining employee, favored the harassed third party.
- The problem of the affair gone sour. Another potential situation is when supervisors and subordinates are involved in

consensual sexual relationships that later turn sour. Obviously, reprimands, demotions, or termination of the subordinate employee after the relationship has ended raises questions. Even when the action taken is warranted, doubt may be cast on the supervisor's decision. If it can be shown that the action was taken as a result of the ending of the relationship, the supervisor has in effect made submission to sexual behavior a condition of employment, i.e., sexual harassment. Such cases illustrate that the potential problems presented by supervisor–subordinate sexual relationships are considerable.

· The mixed-motive problem. When adverse personnel action is taken partly because the employee has refused the advances of the supervisor and partly because of actual poor job performance, the issue is confounded further. If an employee can show that he or she had not been warned before about poor job performance, and that he or she was fired or otherwise negatively treated after rejecting the supervisor's advance, a claim of sexual harassment may well exist.

When an employee is compelled to leave a job in order to avoid harassment or discrimination, the "quit" has essentially become a "fire." In such cases, the resignation may constitute a "constructive discharge," meaning the employee has chosen to quit the job to escape employment practices or conditions that are in violation of equal employment or labor laws. Sexual harassment poses enormous dangers in this respect because employees choose to quit rather than stay on the job, complain, and hope that the problem will be solved. The employer may not know that the harassment is occurring until a former employee no longer fears the consequences of complaining and files suit. Constructive discharge can involve not only unemployment compensation but back pay, court costs, and attorneys' fees.

So what, if anything, will bring about the end of this serious problem? There are at least three factors that could contribute to the elimination of sexual harassment. First, women and men victims must treat harassment as an intolerable working condition and seek whatever formal recourse exists. Second, the work force must become fully integrated, with both sexes having an equal share of jobs, rights, and responsibilities throughout work settings. Third, there must be an overall reorientation of male and female sex roles in this society.

Stereotypical sex roles are damaging to men and women in all phases of life. When both are allowed to break out of traditional, narrow, and confining roles, sexual harassment—which is bred chiefly by inequality and misunderstanding—will cease to occur. Its very existence as a public issue will bring about its end.

9

Food for Thought

The information on the following pages is to help you gain a deeper understanding of sexual harassment. Some of the material is to provide more information, and some material is to make you work and think.

The exercises can be used by individuals alone or in group workshops and training sessions. You will find the exercises more valuable if you discuss your answers with someone else and compare your answers.

Remember, the purpose of the exercises is not to get the right answer, but to gain insight and understanding into the problem of sexual harassment.

GETTING STARTED

These questions are to get you started thinking about some aspects of sexual harassment that you might not have thought about before.

It has been said that sexual harassment is difficult to define. It may range from sexual innuendoes made at inappropriate times, perhaps in the guise of humor, to coerced sexual relations. Harassment is distinct from acceptable flirting; however, on occasion this line may be difficult to draw.

˛ What do you think sexual harassment is?

What do you think some of the consequences of sexual harassment are?

What would you do if you observed a worker being sexually harassed or if someone complained to you of being sexually harassed?

What do you think might be some of the causes of sexual harassment?

SEXUAL HARASSMENT: YES OR NO?

1. Jack overheard two of his co-workers, Sharon and Michael, laughing quietly, whispering, and flirting with each other. The next time he passed Sharon, Jack winked and said, "Hi, sweet thing," and looked her over, all in a joking manner. Sharon was angry and offended and told him so. Did Jack harass Sharon?

2. When Tom gets his work group together for their monthly planning session, he always asks Marilyn to take notes and handle the refreshments. His work group consists of three administrative assistants—Marilyn, James, and Frank. Is Tom harassing Marilyn?

3. Throughout the day, Bob has to drop by the job site to oversee the work of his crew, which is made up of three women and eight men. When he passes Kathy or Shirley he occasionally pats one of them or gives them a "little pinch" or a hug. He has never said anything really sexual to either of them, and they've never objected to his occasional touches. Is he harassing the women?

4. Charlie really likes his employees, and he makes it a point to treat everyone the same. He especially likes to joke and tease in what he feels is a good-natured way. He makes comments like "How's your love life?" and "Don't get any on ya," but Charlie would never be lewd or offensive. None of his employees has ever objected, and sometimes they laugh. Is this sexual harassment?

5. Last night Roger went to a dinner business meeting arranged by his boss, Marie. He expected the whole office staff to be there, but it was just the two of them, and the restaurant was dimly lit, with a very romantic atmosphere. After a few drinks Roger realized that the only business to be discussed was Marie's attraction to him. Just before suggesting that they go to her house for a nightcap, she mentioned the promotion Roger was applying for. Is she sexually harassing Roger?

6. Martha is very attracted to her boss, Dan. Since they're both single, she asked him over for dinner one Friday evening. After a very pleasant evening and a few too many drinks, they ended up spending the night together. Could this be considered sexual harassment?

Answers

1. No. It would be more appropriate to label this *potential* sexual harassment. It is subtle behavior and would not necessarily be called harassment the first time it occurred. However, Jack should not repeat the behavior in any form since Sharon has told him that she is offended by it.

2. No, not technically, though some people think of this as gender harassment—that Tom is harassing her by repeatedly asking her to make coffee because she is a woman. It's better to think of this example in terms of a *discriminatory job assignment*—unless there is a legitimate reason for her always to be selected for coffee making, such as less seniority or being in a

lower job category than the two men. The claim that she likes to handle the refreshments, that she has not complained, or that she makes better coffee is not a sound reason to engage in what appears to be stereotyping.

3. Based on the limited information given in this example, yes. Bob's behavior is physical, looks suspiciously sexual ("little pinches"— where?!), is directed only at two of the women—but only at women and not at men— is repeated, and is done by a supervisor. The fact that the women have not spoken up doesn't carry much weight. Remember, the more severe the behavior, the less responsibility the receiver has to speak up. Bob is supposed to know better than to do this in the first place.

4. Most likely this is an example of subtle sexual harassment. Charlie is a supervisor engaging in this behavior with his subordinates, male and female, but the statement that "sometimes they laugh" can indicate that sometimes they don't laugh because they don't like it. He may be harassing both men and women, even unintentionally. Charlie needs to be told that this is inappropriate behavior.

5. Yes. Marie has made it clear that there is a connection between Roger's response to her invitation and his getting a promotion. This is an example of quid pro quo harassment, and whether Roger likes or appreciates Marie's offer makes no difference.

6. No, but as one person in a workshop said, it should be considered "dumb and dangerous." Supervisors and their subordinates' getting involved romantically is not a good idea. It sets up a situation with all sorts of potential problems in the future, among them sexual harassment.

CASE STUDY 1

You supervise a group of seven laborers, six men and one woman. The woman, Kate, is a new employee and is the first woman to join the work crew. She was hired three months ago.

Until two weeks ago you were very pleased with Kate's work. She was willing and able to take on additional responsibilities when asked and seemed to be getting along well with all the men. But now you're thinking you may have misjudged her. Lately her work hasn't been up to par. She leaves out tools that should be put away, has overlooked some safety standards, and has called in sick three times in two weeks. When you talked with her about it, she seemed distracted and said she would try to improve.

You've also noticed that one of the men on the crew, Les, spends a lot of time with Kate. You overheard him telling her a dirty joke one day, but she smiled and seemed to find it funny. On another occasion you heard him make a comment about her figure, to her face and in front of the other men.

Les can sometimes be what the men call "obnoxious," but everyone likes him and puts up with it. Kate hasn't complained to you, but you feel uneasy about the whole situation.

Questions for discussion:

Do you think sexual harassment has occurred in this situation? Why or why not?

What is your responsibility as a supervisor? Should you wait for Kate to object or speak to you, or should you take action based on what you've seen?

Do you need more information? How would you go about getting it?

What will you do about Kate's job performance?

CASE STUDY 2

Allison went to her supervisor's boss, the group manager, with a complaint about her supervisor, George. She said that George has been sexually harassing her by patting her on the bottom and suggesting that she show him if "blondes really have more fun."

She said that he has done such things to other women and everybody knows it has been going on for years. When the manager asked Allison who else was harassed, she refused to give names, saying that the others were afraid to speak up. She said she was just now coming forward because it seemed to be getting worse and happening more often. As an example, she said that earlier in the week George had tried to pull her into the men's locker room when no one else was around.

The manager was surprised, since George had been with the company for years and was an excellent employee. He immediately called George in and, with Allison present, confronted him with her allegations.

George denied everything. He said she was a liar and a troublemaker and had had "it in for me" since he gave her a poor performance review in the fall. He asked who else had complained, and when the manager said no one, he cited that as proof that Allison was making up the story.

George said he would talk to his attorney about filing charges of slander and stormed out of the office. The manager informed Allison that she would receive a letter of reprimand in her personnel file for making "a frivolous and malicious" complaint.

Questions for discussion:

Did the manager take appropriate action? If not, what else should he have done?

Without action, what is the likely outcome of this situation?

SEXUAL HARASSMENT STUDIES

Numerous studies have been conducted on sexual harassment. Some of the findings are:

Working Smart Newsletter: 51.2 percent experienced sexual harassment; 49.6 percent were harassed in the last two years; 47.8 percent said harassment was overt; 32 percent reported it. 1991.

Merit System Protection Board: A survey of federal employees (more than 8,000 respondents) in 1988 said 42 percent of the women and 14 percent of the men reported having been sexually harassed in the past two years. In a 1979–80 survey (19,500 respondents), 42 percent of the women and 15 percent of the men said they had been harassed. Harassing behavior ranged from unwanted sexual teasing to pressure for sexual favors, and was from co-workers more often than from supervisors. The most common response from victims was doing nothing or ignoring the harassment. U.S. Government, 1980, 1988.

Redbook magazine: Their survey, one of the earliest, said 88 percent (of 9,000 women) had experienced sexual harassment. Half had been fired or knew someone who had been fired for sexual reasons. 1976.

National Law Journal: 60 percent of women attorneys (of 918 respondents) said sexual harassment at work was a major problem: unwanted sexual attention, touching, pinching, comments, looks, gestures, and sexual remarks from supervisors (36 percent), colleagues (30 percent), and clients (32 percent). 1989.

U.S. armed forces: In a Pentagon survey of 20,000 military personnel, 64 percent of the women and 17 percent of the men said they had been sexually harassed. In a Navy study (6,700 surveyed worldwide), 75 percent of the women and 50 percent of the men said harassment occurred within their commands. Pentagon, 1990; Navy, 1991.

Working Woman magazine: A survey of Fortune 500 companies showed that 90 percent have received sexual harassment complaints, more than a third have been sued at least once, and nearly one fourth have been sued repeatedly. A typical large firm will lose $6.7 million per year from lost productivity, absenteeism, and turnover from harassment. 1988.

COSTS OF SEXUAL HARASSMENT

Losing a sexual harassment suit is as costly and damaging as losing any other kind of EEOC action. Courts are awarding money for back pay, reinstatement, unemployment compensation, and attorneys' fees.

In some cases complainants are co-joining their antidiscrimination complaints with state tort actions; in community-property states the suit can name not only the organization and the alleged harasser but also the harasser's spouse. A few examples:

Jean Jew v. *University of Iowa*, August 1990, U.S. District Court. The university was ordered to pay a female professor a total of $1,070,000—$50,000 in back pay, $125,000 in damages, and $895,000 in fees and expenses—ending a five-year court battle. The university's president also publicly apologized to the professor.

Nunez v. *Eskanos and Adler*, October 1990, Alameda County Superior Court, California. A jury awarded $480,000 to a former law clerk who charged that the firm did nothing when she accused her supervisor of raping and sexually harassing her. The award is believed to be the largest to a single plaintiff in the history of California sexual harassment cases.

Plaintiff v. *Seattle City Light*, 1989, Washington State Superior Court. The judge ordered the city electric utility to pay $157,000 for a former employee's attorneys' fees, in addition to a $313,000 jury award for damages and $15,000 for litigation costs to be paid by the chief surveyor and the utility.

Hanson v. *Southern Pacific Railroad*, 1988, Los Angeles County Superior Court. A jury awarded $260,000 to a female journeyman electrician who alleged that her employer failed to maintain a work environment free of sexual harassment. The settlement offered was $35,000; the plaintiff had asked for $100,000.

Paty v. *Puget Sound Bank*, May 1984, U.S. District Court, Washington. A jury awarded the plaintiff $500,000: $50,000 for defamation and $450,000 for discrimination. The judge ruled that the plaintiff might also be entitled to as much as $40,000 in back pay. The case was settled for an undisclosed amount prior to appeal.

Arnold v. *City of Seminole, Oklahoma*, February 1986. The city agreed to a settlement, paying Arnold $235,000, promoting her to lieutenant, clearing her personnel file, and developing policies and procedures to prevent future harassment. The city said higher property taxes might pay for the settlement.

About the Author

Susan L. Webb is a consultant and trainer specializing in the area of human relations. She has researched, designed, and presented workshops and seminars on leadership, supervisory skills, team building, sexual and racial harassment, stress management, and the changing roles of men and women in the work force.

Since 1981, more than 3,000 companies and organizations have used her training programs, publications, or consulting services to stop and prevent harassment in the workplace. Ms. Webb has trained more than 60,000 employees throughout the United States in the area of sexual harassment. She travels extensively, lecturing on other management issues as well.

Ms. Webb has written three books and numerous articles and has been featured in many national professional journals, newspapers, magazines, and broadcasts, including *Time,* the *New York Times, NBC Nightly News,* the *Christian Science Monitor,* National Public Radio, *Forbes, Working Woman, Management Review, Industry Week, Training Magazine,* and *Personnel Administrator.* She is editor of *The Webb Report,* a national newsletter on sexual harassment. She frequently consults and provides expert witness testimony on the subject of sexual harassment and conducts investigations into allegations of harassment and other interpersonal conflicts.

Ms. Webb received her Bachelor's degree in Economics and a Master's degree in Human Relations from the University of Oklahoma. She established Pacific Resource Development Group in 1981 to fill a need for high-quality training and consulting services.

Ms. Webb lives with her husband in Seattle.

Additional copies of *Step Forward: Sexual Harassment in the Workplace—What You Need to Know!* may be ordered by sending a check for $9.95 (please add the following for postage and handling: $2.00 for the first copy, $1.00 for each added copy) to:

MasterMedia Limited
17 East 89th Street
New York, NY 10128
(212) 260-5600
(800) 334-8232
(212) 348-2020 (fax)

Susan L. Webb is available for keynotes and seminars. Please contact MasterMedia's Speakers' Bureau for availability and fee arrangements. Call Tony Colao at (908) 359-1612.

THE PREGNANCY AND MOTHERHOOD DIARY: Planning the First Year of Your Second Career, by Susan Schiffer Stautberg, is the first and only undated appointment diary that shows how to manage pregnancy and career. ($12.95 spiralbound)

CITIES OF OPPORTUNITY: Finding the Best Place to Work, Live and Prosper in the 1990's and Beyond, by Dr. John Tepper Marlin, explores the job and living options for the next decade and into the next century. This consumer guide and handbook, written by one of the world's experts on cities, selects and features forty-six American cities and metropolitan areas. ($13.95 paper, $24.95 cloth)

THE DOLLARS AND SENSE OF DIVORCE, The Financial Guide for Women, by Judith Briles, is the first book to combine practical tips on overcoming the legal hurdles with planning before, during, and after divorce ($10.95 paper)

OUT THE ORGANIZATION: How Fast Could You Find a New Job?, by Madeleine and Robert Swain, is written for the millions of Americans whose jobs are no longer safe, whose companies are not loyal, and who face futures of uncertainty. It gives advice on finding a new job or starting your own business. ($11.95 paper, $17.95 cloth)

AGING PARENTS AND YOU: A Complete Handbook to Help You Help Your Elders Maintain a Healthy, Productive and Independent Life, by Eugenia Anderson-Ellis and Marsha Dryan, is a complete guide to providing care to aging relatives. It gives practical advice and resources to the adults who are helping their elders lead productive and independent lives. ($9.95 paper)

CRITICISM IN YOUR LIFE: How to Give It, How to Take It, How to Make It Work for You, by Dr. Deborah Bright, offers practical advice, in an upbeat, readable, and realistic fashion, for turning criticism into control. Charts and diagrams guide the reader into managing criticism from bosses, spouses, children, friends, neighbors, and in-laws. ($9.95 paper, $17.95 cloth)

BEYOND SUCCESS: How Volunteer Service Can Help You Begin Making a Life Instead of Just a Living, by John F. Raynolds III and Eleanor Raynolds, CBE, is a unique how-to book targeted at business and professional people considering volunteer work, senior citizens who wish to fill leisure time meaningfully, and students trying out various career options. The book is filled with interviews with celebrities, CEOs, and average citizens who talk about the benefits of service work. ($9.95 paper, $19.95 cloth)

MANAGING IT ALL: Time-Saving Ideas for Career, Family, Relationships and Self, by Beverly Benz Treuille and Susan Schiffer Stautberg, is written for women who are juggling careers and families. Over two hundred career women (ranging from a TV anchorwoman to an investment banker) were interviewed. The book contains many humorous anecdotes on saving time and improving the quality of life for self and family. ($9.95 paper)

REAL LIFE 101: The Graduate's Guide to Survival, by Susan Kleinman, supplies welcome advice to those facing "real life" for the first time, focusing on work, money, health, and how to deal with freedom and responsibility. ($9.95 paper)

YOUR HEALTHY BODY, YOUR HEALTHY LIFE: How to Take Control of Your Medical Destiny, by Donald B. Louria, M.A., provides precise advice and strategies that will help you to live a long and healthy life. Learn also about nutrition, exercise, vitamins, and medication, as well as how to control risk factors for major diseases. ($12.95 paper)

THE CONFIDENCE FACTOR: How Self-Esteem Can Change Your Life, by Judith Briles, is based on a nationwide survey of six thousand men and women. Briles explores why women so often feel a lack of self-confidence and have a poor opinion of themselves. She offers step-by-step advice on becoming the person you want to be. ($18.95 cloth)

THE SOLUTION TO POLLUTION: 101 Things You Can Do to Clean Up Your Environment, by Laurence Sombke, offers step-by-step techniques on how to conserve more energy, start a recycling center, choose biodegradable products, and proceed with individual environmental cleanup projects. ($7.95 paper)

TAKING CONTROL OF YOUR LIFE: The Secrets of Successful Enterprising Women, by Gail Blanke and Kathleen Walas, is based on the authors' professional experience with Avon Products' Women of Enterprise Awards, given each year to outstanding women entrepreneurs. The authors offer a specific plan to help you gain control over your life and include business tips and quizzes as well as beauty and lifestyle information. ($17.95 cloth)

SIDE-BY-SIDE STRATEGIES: How Two-Career Couples Can Thrive in the Nineties, by Jane Hershey Cuozzo and S. Diane

Graham, describes how two-career couples can learn the difference between competing with a spouse and becoming a supportive power partner. ($10.95 paper)

DARE TO CONFRONT! How to Intervene When Someone You Care About Has an Alcohol or Drug Problem, by Bob Wright and Deborah George Wright, shows the reader how to use the step-by-step methods of professional interventionists to motivate drug-dependent people to accept the help they need. ($17.95 cloth)

WORK WITH ME! How to Make the Most of Office Support Staff, by Betsy Lazary, shows how to find, train, and nurture the "perfect" assistant and how best to utilize your support staff professionals. ($9.95 paper)

MANN FOR ALL SEASONS: Wit and Wisdom from The Washington Post's *Judy Mann*, by Judy Mann, shows the columnist at her best as she writes about women, families, and the politics of the women's revolution. ($9.95 paper, $19.95 cloth)

THE SOLUTION TO POLLUTION IN THE WORKPLACE, by Laurence Sombke, Terry M. Robertson, and Elliot M. Kaplan, supplies employees with everything they need to know about cleaning up their workspace, including recycling, using energy efficiently, conserving water, and buying recycled products and nontoxic supplies. ($9.95 paper)

THE ENVIRONMENTAL GARDENER: The Solution to Pollution for Lawns and Gardens, by Laurence Sombke, focuses on what each of us can do to protect our endangered plant life. A practical sourcebook and shopping guide. ($8.95 paper)

THE LOYALTY FACTOR: Building Trust in Today's Workplace, by Carol Kinsey Goman, Ph.D., offers techniques for restoring commitment and loyalty in the workplace. ($9.95 paper)

DARE TO CHANGE YOUR JOB—AND YOUR LIFE, by Carole Kanchier, Ph.D., provides a look at career growth and development throughout the life cycle. ($10.95 paper)

MISS AMERICA: In Pursuit of the Crown, by Ann-Marie Bivans, is an authorized guidebook to the Pageant, containing eyewitness accounts, complete historical data, and a realistic look at the trials and triumphs of potential Miss Americas. ($27.50 cloth)

POSITIVELY OUTRAGEOUS SERVICE: New and Easy Ways to Win Customers for Life, by T. Scott Gross, identifies what the consumers of the nineties really want and how businesses can develop effective marketing strategies to answer those needs. ($14.95 paper)

BREATHING SPACE: Living and Working at a Comfortable Pace in a Sped-Up Society, by Jeff Davidson, helps readers to handle information and activity overload and gain greater control over their lives. ($10.95 paper)

TWENTYSOMETIIING: Managing and Motivating Today's New Work Force, by Lawrence J. Bradford, Ph.D., and Claire Raines, M.A., examines the work orientation of the younger generation, offering managers in businesses of all kinds a practical guide to better understand and supervise their young employees. ($22.95 cloth)

BALANCING ACTS! Juggling Love, Work, Family and Recreation, by Susan Schiffer Stautberg and Marcia L. Worthing, provides strategies to achieve a balanced life by reordering priorities and setting realistic goals. ($12.95 paper)

Also Available from the Author

Sexual Harassment: Investigator's Manual
Sexual Harassment: Training Package
Guidelines for Managers, Supervisors, and Employees
Six Simple Steps to Stop Sexual Harassment
25 Things to Do If Sexual Harassment Happens to You
How to Handle Sexual Harassment Complaints
Sexual Harassment: Shades of Gray (video)
The Webb Report (monthly newsletter)

To order, to receive a catalogue, or to get information about becoming a certified Shades of Gray consultant and distributor, call Premiere Publishing, Ltd., (800) 767-3062.